Praise for *Living With Bears Handbook*

"Each year thousands of bears are destroyed in North America largely because of our carelessness. Use this excellent book and you can help ensure the bear has a wild future in our increasingly human-dominated world."

Beth Pratt-Bergstrom, California Director, National Wildlife Federation and author of *When Mountain Lions are Neighbors*

"I couldn't ask for a better reference. *Living With Bears Handbook* covers everything people need to know in an interesting, motivating, easy-to-understand way; I recommend it to anyone who lives and recreates in bear country and to those who need a tool to reach them."

Jaime L. Sajecki, Black Bear Project Leader,
Virginia Department of Game and Inland Fisheries

"The best single source of information and inspiration on how to understand and live compatibly with bears. Linda Masterson writes with understanding, authority and wit, and invites readers to share in her encyclopedic knowledge of bears and how to reduce human-bear conflicts."

Stephen Herrero, Professor Emeritus of Environmental Science, University of Calgary, Canada, and author of *Bear Attacks: Their Causes and Avoidance*

"*Living With Bears Handbook* is the most comprehensive, cogent, and handy guide about bears that I've found. I recommend this book as essential reading for our young officers in training and to citizens who live and play in Colorado's abundant bear country."

Jerry A. Apker, Wildlife Manager, Colorado Parks and Wildlife

"A remarkable book that will change the way you think and act in bear country. Linda Masterson is a master writer and researcher. Her book should be on the shelves of every library and in every home by which a bear has ever strolled."

Sylvia Dolson, Executive Director, Get Bear Smart Society

"An excellent source of information for the general public and management biologists on the biology of bears, the underlying causes of human-bear conflicts and methods for reducing conflicts where people live, work and recreate in bear habitats. I heartily recommend this book."

John J. Beecham, Ph.D., International Union for the Conservation of Nature

"Linda makes it easy to be part of the solution."

Rachel Mazur, Wildlife Ecologist and author of *Speaking of Bears*

"*Living With Bears Handbook* will help readers become an effective partner in keeping bears wild, healthy and a part of our landscape for years to come."

Colleen Olfenbuttel, for *International Bear News*
Bear Biologist, North Carolina Wildlife Resources Commission

"An excellent job of presenting a great deal of valuable information that promotes coexistence. I highly recommend it to everyone living in bear country, and wildlife managers who deal with human-bear conflicts."

John Hechtel, Bear Biologist, Alaska Department of Fish and Game

"Easy to understand, fun to read, and full of case histories that present practical solutions to a variety of real-life human-bear conflicts. As a conflict resolution specialist, I'll refer many people to *Living With Bears Handbook*."

Patti Sowka, IUCN Human-Bear Conflict Expert Team

"Bravo! This go-to handbook pulls together a comprehensive collection of facts and practical advice on living with bears. A fun and insightful read."

Hank Hristienko, Black Bear, Moose & Wolf Manager, Manitoba Conservation

"A copy of this book should be in the door pocket of every agency official who deals with human-bear conflicts and gives a damn about bears."

Chris Parmeter, District Wildlife Manager, Colorado Parks and Wildlife

"A requisite for anyone living or recreating in bear habitat, and an exceptional resource for those of us who work with bears professionally that knowledgeably addresses both the issues and the solutions. Now if people will just emulate what Linda is teaching, our world will be much happier for humans and bears alike."

Carl Lackey, Game Biologist, Nevada Department of Wildlife

"This highly readable handbook will be a valuable resource to anyone trying to understand or manage human-bear conflicts."

Marty Obbard, Ontario Ministry of Natural Resources and Forestry

"This handbook is the definitive resource I refer to when training volunteers or presenting to the public. It provides all the tools necessary for people living and recreating in bear country to share habitat with our wild neighbors."

Mary K. McCormac, Education and Watchable Wildlife Coordinator,
Colorado Parks and Wildlife

LIVING WITH Bears HANDBOOK

EXPANDED 2ND EDITION

Linda Masterson

Foreword by Rich Beausoleil

PIXYJACK PRESS INC

Living With Bears Handbook, Expanded 2nd Edition

Published by PixyJack Press, Inc.
PO Box 149, Masonville, CO 80541 USA
www.PixyJackPress.com

print ISBN 978-1-936555-61-1
Kindle ISBN 978-1-936555-62-8
epub ISBN 978-1-936555-63-5

Library of Congress Cataloging-in-Publication Data

Masterson, Linda (Linda J.)
[Living with bears]
Living with bears handbook / Linda Masterson ; foreword by Rich Beausoleil.
-- Expanded 2nd edition.
pages cm
"1st edition: Living with bears : a practical guide to bear country, c2006."--T.p. verso of galley.
Includes bibliographical references and index.
Summary: "A practical resource for understanding bear biology and behavior, why human-bear conflicts are on the rise, and what we can do at home, at play, and in our communities to coexist with black bears and reduce problems that come from sharing space"
-- Provided by publisher.
ISBN 978-1-936555-61-1
1. Black bear--Behavior. 2. Bear attacks--North America--Prevention. 3. Human-animal relationships--North America. I. Title.
QL737.C27M3522 2006
599.78'5--dc23
2015034099

1st Edition: *Living With Bears: A Practical Guide to Bear Country*, © 2006

Photos: Front cover bears by Bill Lea; backyard bears on the back cover by Paul Conrad. Unless noted otherwise, bear photos from various photo agencies or the author. Book design by LaVonne Ewing. Beartoon illustrations by Sara Tuttle.

More info at: ***www.LivingWithBears.com***

CAUTION TO READERS: PixyJack Press, Linda Masterson, Rich Beausoleil and the dozens of bear experts and organizations from the U.S. and Canada who consulted on or provided information for this book assume no liability for accidents, injuries, or property damage caused by bears. Understanding and following the recommendations provided in this book will lessen the likelihood of a bear encounter that results in injury, death or property damage, but bears are individuals, and much like people, there is no way to predict or ensure the specific behavior of an individual bear under all circumstances. Every effort has been made to assure the accuracy of the information in this book. The publisher and author cannot be held responsible for any errors.

For the bears, and for everyone trying to improve human-bear relations.

And for my husband Cory, my partner in all things great and small.

CONTENTS

continued

APPENDIX

FOREWORD

Over the past 20 years, I have been asked tens of thousands of times why human-bear conflicts occur. The answer isn't because bears are troublemakers, or bear populations are out of control, or because they enjoy being around people. And while a poor year for natural food source production often results in increased sightings, there is a much simpler explanation. Bears come into conflict with people because we give them a reason to. We attract them with the endless supply of high-calorie food sources we intentionally or unintentionally provide.

If blame needs to be assigned, don't blame a bear for having an unmatched sense of smell, or for taking advantage of an available food source that will help it or its family survive, or even for outsmarting people. Blame the source of the attractant; it's not the bear that's being a nuisance. *Merriam-Webster* defines an attractive nuisance as: something on one's property that poses a risk to children or others who may be attracted to it. It's all those things that people seldom think about, from garbage to bird feeders to fruit trees, that can be deadly attractants to bears.

Working with bears is an incredibly rewarding profession, but it is not without its non-biological challenges. It does include research, ecology, biology, and trying to build responsible data-driven management plans. But it also involves mastering politics, economics, sociology, recreation and conflict resolution. And most of all, it requires working with people, from homeowners and communities to politicians and land developers and just about everyone who lives or works or visits or has any interests in areas where bears are present. The cast of characters is always changing. That's why we all get asked the same questions and deal with the same problems hundreds of thousands of times.

I often say that educating people about human-bear conflict prevention is the heart disease of wildlife management. We all know that to live a healthy lifestyle and avoid heart disease we need to eat well and exercise. But all too often it takes a heart attack before someone finally changes their behavior and does what it takes to prevent any more problems. The same is true with human-bear conflicts. Most people know that bears will eagerly take advantage of any food sources people provide, but instead of removing attractants, people look the other way until one of those bear visits results in property damage or even injury. Bears are really smart, and tend to repeat successful behavior. So waiting to report a problem and remove the attractant(s) makes it much more challenging to do what it takes to prevent additional conflicts. That's why so much of wildlife management is actually people management.

When Linda asked me to be a part of this book, I accepted her invitation without hesitation. Why? Because in my work I try my best to always operate under the rule that I can be part of the problem or be part of the solution; I know this book follows the latter. I always thought the original version of *Living With Bears* was well done, and it quickly became my go-to book. I left it on my desk and would frequently use it as a reference when people called or the media needed quick and to-the-point advice. I also took it to public education events I was involved with and recommended it to people interested in learning more about human-bear conflict.

In this revised edition, Linda has once again spent an enormous amount of time researching the scientific literature, establishing and maintaining dialogue with respected bear biologists across North America, and distilling an incredible amount of information down to the most pertinent educational, actionable messages for anyone interested in being part of the real solution of stopping the cycle of human-bear conflict. Besides all that, it's a fun read.

This second edition of *Living With Bears* has been completely reorganized and updated, and I think it makes it an even more useful book. I'm proud to be a part of it; it will prominently occupy that go-to space on my desk, on top of the stack.

As the human population increases and bear habitat becomes more constricted, human-bear conflicts will likely become more common until people make a concerted effort to change. If you appreciate bears in any way, I hope you will read this book, put it to use, and share it with your family and friends; heck, spread the word on social media if you can, because the solution to this epidemic lies within.

I look forward to the day the trend reverses and human-bear conflicts decrease every year, rather than the opposite. Then, I won't have to continue to watch animals I respect so greatly be needlessly killed because of their intelligence and resourcefulness; that's not why I got into this profession.

Ultimately, the essential and lasting solutions won't come from management agencies, they will come from people. If you apply yourself and work with others to prevent human-bear conflicts, I know you can make a difference and I know you can affect change, for people and for bears.

Rich Beausoleil

Bear & Cougar Specialist
Washington Department of Fish and Wildlife

© Paul Conrad

PROLOGUE

"Bears can't read.
Only people can prevent problems with bears."

That's how I've been signing off my emails since 2006, when the first edition of *Living With Bears* was published. I've learned a lot more about both people and bears since then.

I now have an even deeper appreciation of bears and an even greater admiration for their intelligence and adaptability. And I am continually amazed at their determination to survive in an ever-expanding world of humans.

I also have a much deeper appreciation of the power of one person to change the planet, because I've had the privilege of getting to know so many dedicated people who are doing just that. From bear researchers and biologists to volunteers and community leaders to dedicated wildlife management agency folks to homeowners and outdoor enthusiasts—good people make a difference every day.

And that's a good thing, because no matter how resourceful bears are, people still rule the world. Only people have the power to step up to the plate and do what it takes to craft a peaceful coexistence with the other inhabitants of the planet.

I hope you're reading this book because you want to be one of those people.

I also hope you'll take time to read the thought-provoking foreword by Washington's long-time and widely respected bear biologist Rich Beausoleil, who spent untold hours serving as my go-to bear guy, tireless fact-checker, and real-world litmus test for all the information in the book. Please read the chapters that explain what bears are all about (I promise they are not boring) before you dive into the information on how to prevent conflicts, avoid confrontations, and live and play smartly and safely in bear country.

Once you understand what makes bears tick, it's a whole lot easier to understand how what you do—or don't do—can make all the difference.

Doing the right thing isn't always easy. But it is always right.

Linda Masterson

Discover the path to better human-bear relations.

The Bear Facts

1

What's the Problem?

Every year in North America thousands of healthy black bears and more than a hundred grizzly bears lose their lives for being too good at making a living in people country.

Ask almost any bear behavior expert what's the biggest cause of human-bear conflicts and the answer is always the same: teaching bears to associate humans with food is a recipe for trouble. Almost all conflicts between people and bears can be traced back to people intentionally or unintentionally attracting or providing food sources for bears.

Bears instinctively avoid us. But foraging all day in the wild is a lot of work, and there are no guarantees of turning in for the night with a full stomach. Foraging for five minutes in the garbage is easy, predictable and productive. Sometimes the lure of a life-sustaining easy meal for very little effort is too powerful to ignore.

Bears are biologically programmed to follow their noses—seven times more powerful than a bloodhound's—to food sources, whether they're around the corner or several miles away.

Nature has equipped bears with the size, strength and endurance to regularly roam far and wide searching for meals, along with the stomach of an omnivore so they can eat just about anything. Bears are naturally curious and constantly exploring their environment looking for new things to eat. That can lead them to new natural food sources—or places it isn't safe for bears to be.

Bears are attracted by anything that smells interesting or different or unusual. It doesn't have to be good to eat, or even edible. Sometimes there are berries or nuts or maybe an ant hill or beehive or rotten log full of insects or even a yummy decomposing carcass at the end of the olfactory rainbow.

But sometimes a bear follows its nose to an overflowing garbage can, a bird feeder filled with seeds, a mini-orchard of ripening fruit, a flock of chickens roaming through the backyard, a picnic table groaning with food, or a backpack stuffed with energy bars. Getting its paws on such calorie-laden rewards teaches the bear that overcoming its natural wariness of people pays off big time. Now the bear will risk spending a few minutes someplace it doesn't really want to be for the reward of a quick and easy meal.

Sometimes the source of the interesting odor turns out to be something that's not edible even by bear standards, like a hot tub cover, vinyl tarp, container of oil or even a citronella candle. Sometimes that good smell turns out to be coming from something like antifreeze that's downright lethal.

It usually starts with something small. If nothing bad happens, the

Michael Seraphin, Colorado Parks & Wildlife

bear learns it's O.K. to come back for more. The next time it won't be so shy or wary. Soon it may be going from house to house or camp to camp looking for handouts. Before you know it the bear has become a "nuisance" and is causing a lot of "problems."

People expect bears to intuitively understand that they're supposed to respect our boundaries and leave our stuff alone. But the only rules bears play by are self-preservation and survival of the fittest.

While most people don't have to worry about where their next meal is coming from, all wild bears live from paw to mouth, with no guarantees where or when they'll find something to eat. So when a bear discovers a seemingly endless supply of high-calorie food, it will come back until the source dries up. It's simple math. A bear foraging out in the woods would have to work all day long to find the same number of calories it can gulp down in minutes in someone's backyard. The less energy bears have to expend finding food, the more fat they can store for their upcoming long winter's fast.

If a hard-working woman struggling against all odds to make a living behaved like a mother bear, we'd greatly admire her. We'd say things like, "No matter how tough life got, she figured out a way to survive, find food for her family, and put a roof over their heads. She worked three jobs, learned new skills, and took some big risks that paid off with big rewards." The family would probably get their own reality TV show and a bunch of lucrative endorsements.

© Michael Burhart, Bear Smart Durango

In the real world it's much more likely the bear will learn to rely on people for food and become human food-conditioned. The more relaxed human food-conditioned bears become around us, the better the chances for conflicts between the two-footed and four-footed neighbors. When human-bear conflicts escalate to encounters and confrontations, it's almost always the bear that loses.

Attract Bears and They Will Come

An elderly resident of North Vancouver, British Columbia, got quite the scare when she went to close her refrigerator door and found a black bear standing on the other side browsing through the selections. The bear put its paw on her hand; when the woman pulled away, her hand was cut. The bear then left by the open back door. The woman received a few stitches. Conservation officers tracked and tranquilized the bear. After it was identified as a food-conditioned bear with a taste for garbage it was killed.

Neighborhood residents had seen the bear trying to get into unnatural food sources earlier in the day, but no one had reported it. A necropsy showed the bear's feces were loaded with garbage, packaging and foil. Authorities say there were attractants both inside and outside the house. Several other incidents had been reported earlier in the week, including two bears that wandered into a home where the doors had been left open and a bear that broke into a garage that was filled with rotting garbage. Wildlife officials said that all the areas experiencing break-ins or walk-ins were along wildlife corridors or areas with natural food sources, where residents and businesses need to take extra care not to attract wildlife.

One Bite Really Will Kill You

If things that look or smell like food are readily available, it's just a matter of time before a bear comes exploring. If the bear has a positive experience (getting a food reward) without any negative consequences (being yelled at and chased off), it will try for what its enterprising bear-brain thinks might be an even bigger and better reward.

People tend to ignore these early stages of conflict, hoping the bear will eventually move on, or rationalizing that losing a bag of garbage or the occasional feeder full of birdseed isn't so bad.

But ignoring a bear's activity encourages it not only to continue, but to escalate. The longer people wait to report conflicts and remove attractants, the more likely it is that some bears will push past the limits of tolerance and destroy property or threaten humans. And when agencies have to choose between the safety of people and the lives of bears, people must come first.

This step-by-step experimentation that starts with stumbling across some sort of human-provided food reward and ends with lights out for the bear is what biologists call "the behavioral ladder of progression."

© Paul Conrad

"We lure bears in with the promise of an easy meal, and then punish them with death for accepting our invitation." — *Sylvia Dolson, Executive Director, Get Bear Smart Society*

The Bear Behavioral Ladder of Progression

A step-by-step journey from wary beginning to untimely end

Smell something interesting. Follow nose to people place. Food smells good, but people might be dangerous. Wait until dark to explore.

Gobble up birdseed on ground. Knock down feeder, eat lots more. Run back to the woods.

Come back a few nights later. Feeder is full again! Chow down. Follow nose onto deck.

Jackpot! Find garbage by back door. Open, scatter and eat. Score a day's worth of calories. Plan to return often to this new food bonanza. Amble back to the woods.

Explore the neighborhood. Get much fatter much faster than you could foraging in the woods.

Start coming during the day since food supply seems endless and humans appear to be harmless.

Find open garage, knock over refrigerator. Eat pizza and ice cream. Score a week's worth of calories.

Do enough damage to get reported. Make the news.

Start approaching people, looking for food. Get trapped, ear-tagged and hauled away.

Find your way back. Yummy treats still there! Pick up where you left off.

Scare someone putting out the trash.

Get labeled a threat to human safety.

Get killed way before your time.

© Derek Reich

And that makes room for another bear that smells something interesting.

BEAR CALORIE COUNTER

Provided by People	Calories
Birdseed, 1 pound black oil sunflower seeds	2,585
Bird feeder filled with 7 pounds of birdseed	18,095
Hummingbird feeder, 32 ounce	3,200
Apples in the orchard, one bushel[1]	6,720
Dry dog food, 3 cups	1,200
Honey, 1 cup	1,024
Beehive[2], ten-frame hive, developing bees & honey	68,672
Chickens (minus feathers), three (the rest got away)	4,500
Eggs, one dozen (eggs can't fly)	888
Cherry pie, cooling on windowsill	2,460
Grab bag snack chips, 2½ ounces	400
Jelly donut	310
Pizza slice	375
Peanut butter & jelly sandwich	490
Bacon grease, ½ cup	936
Chocolate chip cookies, 1-pound package	3,200
Fried chicken, 10-piece bucket	2,735
Picnic basket, left on table[3]	9,510
Cooler, left under table[4]	6,536

[1] A bushel of apples weighs about 42 pounds. A mature dwarf apple tree produces an average yield of 1 to 6 bushels of apples. One Red Delicious apple is about 110 calories.

[2] Beehive with 10 deep frames of brood: 40 pounds of honey (54 cups) yields 55,296 calories; approximately 66,800 developing bees (larva and pupae) at 2.5 calories per gram yields 13,376 calories, for a total calorie load of 68,672.

[3] Picnic basket: one package hot dog buns, one box of graham crackers, 4 chocolate bars, 16-oz. bag of potato chips, 14 oz. package of Oreos, a bag of marshmallows.

[4] Cooler: one pound of hot dogs, one pound of potato salad, one 12-pack of regular beer, two 2-liter bottles of soda, one 16-oz container of chip dip.

Provided by Nature	Calories
Huckleberries, 1 pound	166
Cranberries, 1 pound	210
Blueberries, 1 pound	256
Raspberries, 1 pound	229
Cherries, 1 pound	288
Acorns (60-80), 1 pound	2,082
Tent Caterpillars, 537 to a pound	430

Food for Thought

To get the 20,000 calories a day needed while fattening up before hibernation, a bear would need to eat 672 acorns, 78 pounds of blueberries, nearly 25,000 tent caterpillars **or ONE 7-pound birdfeeder filled with black oil sunflower seeds**.

An industrious mama bear teaching her cub to play climb for calories. The feeder was empty, but still smelled like birdseed. *© Carol Dollard*

Dead End Ahead

It took a three-year-old bear in Montana about a month to go from shy and wary of humans to a statistic.

An elderly couple in the Ashland area first noticed the bear hanging around their corrals. Soon it was nosing around the house. Then one day the bear got into their pickup truck and helped itself to the garbage in the back. As time went by the bear got a little more comfortable around them. Eventually its super-sensitive nose led it to the bowl of cat food on the patio by the back door. It gobbled down the calories and soon came back looking for more.

One day the bear peeked in an open window and a few minutes later surprised the couple in the living room. The man, who was in his 80s, kicked and cussed at the bear until it finally found the open window and escaped. But the next day the bear was back. Fearful of what might happen next, the man shot it. Then they called the game warden.

This whole sad situation could probably have been prevented if they'd started cussing the bear back when it first started nosing around the corrals, quit feeding the cats outside, locked up their garbage and removed whatever else attracted the bear in the first place.

What's the Solution?

Most human-bear conflicts can be prevented, if people will be half as adaptable and resourceful as bears. Bears are extremely flexible thinkers. Once they learn the rules, as long as natural food sources, mates and denning spaces are available, most bears can be taught that it's in their best interests to avoid people places.

People are supposed to be smarter than bears, but we often seem both less adaptable and less willing to change our lifestyles and habits. Appreciating wildlife and caring about the environment is good. But it's changing how we live, play and think that will make a real difference for both people and bears. ❖

2

Where the Bears Are

Where do black bears live? As one bear researcher succinctly put it, "Anywhere they can."

According to the latest status reports, black bear populations can now be found in 42 U.S. states and throughout most of Canada. There's also an increasing black bear population in parts of Mexico, although there's no reliable population estimate.

© Bill Levy

How Many Bears Are There?

The total U.S. bear population, excluding Alaska, is estimated at somewhere north of 300,000. The number of black bears in Alaska hasn't been officially documented, but most experts put it between 100,000 and 200,000. An estimated 450,000 black bears live in Canada. That adds up to 850,000 to 950,000 black bears throughout North America.

"On a difficulty scale of 1 to 10, estimating bear population size is an 11," says bear biologist Rich Beausoleil. "Bears don't travel in herds or live in places they can be easily observed. And bears have overlapping ranges that vary widely in size. Because capturing bears and estimating populations is difficult, researchers need large sample sizes, so they often work in the areas with the highest densities. If those results are applied uniformly across the state, bear numbers can be overestimated."

Bear and People Populations Expanding

The agency survey conducted for the 2015 Eastern and Western Black Bear Workshops revealed that 31 percent of states and 25 percent of Canadian provinces believed their bear populations were expanding. The number of resident bears estimated ranged from a mere 10 in Rhode Island to more than 100,000 in Alaska and Ontario, Canada. Many agencies lack the scientific data to state with any certainty whether bear populations are stable, decreasing or increasing, so they list the population trend as "unknown." For a look at bear populations in your state or province, check out the chart in the appendix.

Human population is much easier to track. The Census Bureau's population clock lists the 2015 population of the U.S. at 321.2 million people. As a nation, we have a net gain of one person every 12 seconds. So with even the current modest annual growth rate of about three-quarters of one percent, the U.S. population grows by more than two million people each year. So no matter how you juggle the numbers, the actual ratio of bears to people drops every year.

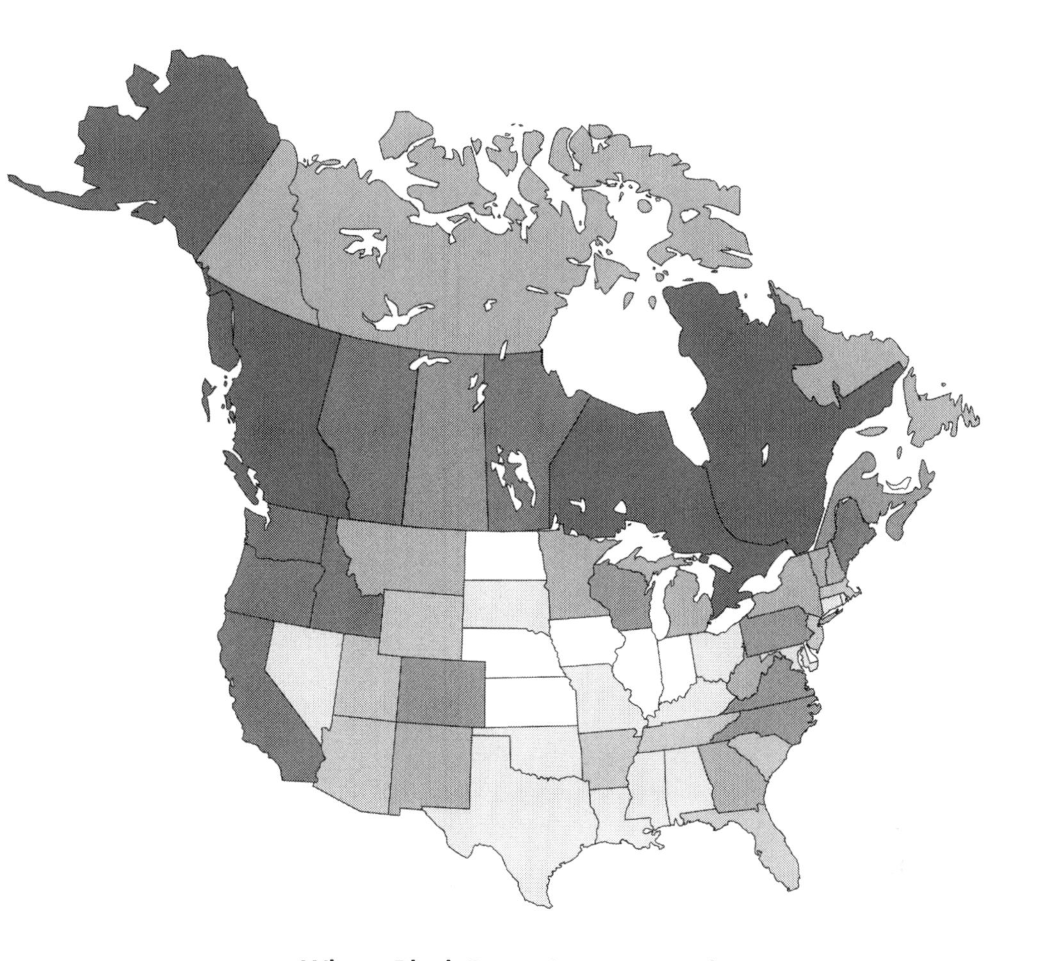

Where Black Bears Can Be Found

According to the latest estimates, between 850,000 and 950,00 black bears roam North America today. Even states without resident bear populations often have bears passing through. Keep in mind that counting bears is not easy. Bears travel long distances, either alone or in small family groups, and generally remain within forest cover so it can be difficult to distinguish one bear from another.

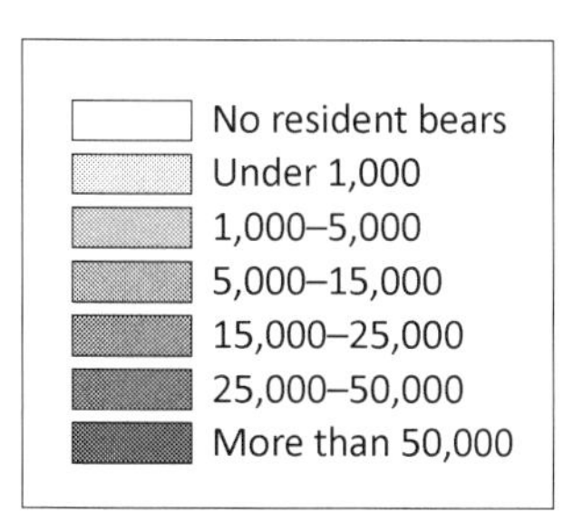

See the appendix for state-by-state details.

But about half of the states report that the number of human-bear conflicts is rising.

Why? The long answer is complicated by several factors, including the attitudes and values of the resident human population, how much outdoor recreation occurs in bear habitat, how many people live full or part time in or close to the areas bears frequent, how agencies record human-bear sightings and interactions, and how accustomed the local human population, including the media, is to living with wildlife.

In places where people aren't used to sharing space with bears, just one bear wandering through a greenbelt can trigger dozens of calls to the agency; those calls could be recorded as anything from 30 sightings to 30 nuisance-bear complaints. Many agencies are now training personnel to do a more accurate job of separating sightings from actual incidents.

The short answer is pretty easy: today there are millions more people living, working and playing in areas where bears can live too.

The human population in the wildland-urban interface, commonly known as the WUI, is booming. Loosely defined, the WUI is where civilization and wildlands overlap. As I'm writing this chapter in 2014 the interface is home to an estimated 120 million people, more than a third of the population of the U.S.

By the time you read this, it will have grown even bigger. Because every year, two million acres of wildlands are turned into places the resident bears must learn to share with the expanding human population. And sparsely populated places that used to be "the country," "the woods," "the mountains," and "the lake" sprout clusters of housing developments that put people in much closer proximity to bears on a daily basis.

There's no end in sight. Experts estimate that to date only about 30 percent of the WUI has been developed.

The population survey conducted for the 2015 Eastern and Western Black Bear Workshops also collected a wide variety of other data, including the number of bear complaints received by agencies and the number of bears killed because of human-bear conflicts. Florida, with about 20 million people and 3,000 bears, leads the list for bear complaints, with an annual average of 5,584. Washington, with just over 7 million people and 25,000 bears, has an average of 529 complaints each year. Or looked at another way, Florida gets about two complaints for every bear; Washington gets one complaint for every 47 bears. On the surface, the numbers can seem confusing, but one thing that's crystal clear is that it's not the number of bears that dictates the number of bear complaints.

Oftentimes people from cities and suburbs who move into bear country are astonished to find they're now sharing space with a variety of four-footed neighbors that can be just as challenging to get along with as the two-footed ones they left behind.

Even locals who've lived in bear country for years often remark that the peaceful coexistence they once enjoyed with the local wildlife isn't so peaceful anymore.

"We've lived here 40 years, and never used to have problems with bears," one Coloradoan lamented. "We're not doing anything any different. What's going on?"

A quick look at the county records revealed the human population of the canyon they live in had grown from a few hundred people to more than 10,000 over that same time period. Streams provide steady sources of water. Chokecherries, serviceberries and wild raspberries crowd the banks. It's a great place to live. It's also a great place to be a bear.

The ursine residents have

The Town of Snowmass Village, Colorado, uses portable sign boards to alert people to bear activity in a particular area.

tried to adapt to the rising tide of humans building homes, planting gardens, raising chickens, and fencing in meadows in the midst of their habitat. But the chances of bears meeting people as they run the human obstacle course in what used to be the bears' backyard have increased a thousand fold. And so have the chances of bears encountering all manner of human-provided food that is now there for the taking.

The quality and quantity of natural foods for bears can vary greatly by season and by year. When high-quality natural foods are scarce, bears find it hard to ignore the abundant, reliable and calorie-packed human food sources.

A Short History of Bears in the U.S.

When Europeans first arrived, black bears could be found wherever there were forests—which was most of the continent except for the Great Plains and the frozen tundra.

Early American pioneers were intent on farming; black bears were just another varmint standing in the way of progress. In the late 1800s wildlife was either a commodity to be used, or a problem to be exterminated. There were no hunting seasons or rules and regulations; bears were plentiful and bounties so common hunters could make a good living selling bear pelts. Hides fetched $8 each, and meat went for eight cents a pound. The concept of wildlife as a resource to be conserved and enjoyed by all was still decades away. By the end of the century black bear populations had been decimated in much of the eastern U.S.

Eventually managing wildlife as a renewable resource replaced exploitation and extermination, and state and federal management agencies were born. Then along came the Industrial Revolution; millions of acres of marginal farmland were abandoned and eventually reclaimed by second-growth forests. As these new forests matured over the next century bears once again had a place to live.

Enlightened conservationists led movements to set aside parks to help preserve and protect our natural resources. Parks offered people unspoiled places to come and experience nature, and provided a safe haven for wildlife. Communities focused on serving the tourists quickly sprouted around the parks. Towns like Gatlinburg, Tennessee, and Estes Park, Colorado, that were once tiny hamlets have grown into sprawling mini-cities with thousands of full-time residents, tens of thousands of part-timers and seasonal employees, and literally millions of visitors.

Today green belts and open spaces are often mandated amenities in new housing developments and communities. These natural areas make excellent travel corridors for wildlife as well as people. But with open land harder and more expensive to come by, greenbelts are seldom large enough to provide a safe harbor for large wildlife species; parks and open spaces with walkways and bike paths going through developed land can actually increase the odds of people and bears encountering each other.

With both bear and human populations on the increase, wildlands shrinking and WUI expanding, there's little doubt that the potential for human-bear interactions, and possible conflicts, will keep going up. So it's up to the humans to prove that more bears plus more people doesn't have to add up to more trouble. ❖

© Warren Bielenberg

Bears Will Find a Way

> "Nevada has no bear, except for an occasional one that strays in along the Sierras adjacent to Lake Tahoe in California. Therefore we have no management responsibilities."
>
> *Nevada Black Bear Status Report*
> *1st Western Black Bear Workshop, 1979*

Thirty years after Director Glen Griffith's 30-second presentation at the first Western Black Bear Workshop in 1979, Nevada hosted the 10th Annual Black Bear Workshop, where I was both a presenter and an attendee.

Today Nevada has one of the highest-profile black bear populations in the country, thanks to the appeal of the Reno/Lake Tahoe area for both bears and people and the variety of ongoing research conducted by the state.

History shows that black bears were once found throughout several Nevada mountain ranges. Bears vanished by the 1900s, but began reappearing in the 1980s. By 1987 bear complaints and sightings were going up faster than either human or bear populations were growing.

A look back reveals that Nevada was virtually stripped of its piñon-juniper woodlands and all of the conifer forests in the Tahoe Basin during the mining boom of the 1800s, back in the age when natural resources were just commodities to be exploited. This wholesale altering of habitat most likely drove bears out of the state.

Theories abound regarding why bears have now returned to much of their historic range, including the popular myth that Yosemite deports its most enterprising bears to Nevada.

"Not true," says Carl Lackey, Nevada's long-time black bear biologist who was the chair of the 2009 Western Black Bear Workshop. "The increase in local bears and bear complaints is a result of expanding bear and human populations coupled with bears' adaptability and skill at taking advantage of carelessly stored human foods."

What really happened? Eventually the opinions about natural resources began to change. Conifer forests and woodlands were protected, and slowly the landscape began to revert to its pre-pillaging stage. As habitat returned, so did bears.

3

Understanding Black Bears

Black bears are powerful and strong enough to attack and kill people, but very seldom do. They could easily defend their young, but are more likely to flee. They're classified as carnivores, but most of their diet is vegetation. They are naturally shy and wary of humans but adaptable and resourceful enough to live among us.

The average bear's life is dedicated to finding food and shelter, propagating the species, and avoiding trouble. Bears have a unique combination of physical and mental characteristics and skills. They're naturally cautious when they encounter anything unfamiliar, a trait

Bears are good hikers, and can roam 5 to 15 miles each day searching for food. *© Jim Conley*

that helps them avoid danger. They're also highly adaptable, insatiably curious, and very intelligent, flexible and resourceful; all attributes that help them survive in a complex and ever-changing world.

Bears are neither the ferocious man-eating beasts of movies, nightmares and sensational "news" stories, nor the cuddly teddy bears of cartoons and story books. Just like humans, bears have both general characteristics and individual temperaments and behavior patterns.

"If you've studied an individual bear, its behavior is almost 100 percent predictable. The bear has developed certain set ways to respond to danger, challenge, opportunity, obstacles," explains noted bear researcher Steve Herrero.

© Bill Lea

A Bear's Life

Bears sometimes live 25 years or more in the wild; average life span varies from region to region. Bears generally mature and mate around age three, but growing up can take a couple of years longer if food is hard to come by.

As it is for most young animals, the world is a dangerous place for little bears, and even with plenty of available food, an average of one in four cubs dies before its first birthday. In bad food years, fewer cubs survive. Predators like mountain lions, wolves, coyotes and adult male bears are thought to be the biggest cause of cub mortality, but cubs also fall out of trees, drown, are hit by cars, and can starve to death if something happens to their mother before they can fend for themselves.

Adult bears do occasionally die of old age, or more rarely of disease, but most bears die from human-related causes: hunting, poaching, the destruction of bears involved in human-bear conflicts, and motor vehicle collisions.

Oldest Known Wild Black Bear

The oldest wild black bear of known age was just shy of her fortieth birthday when she died of natural causes in northern Minnesota sometime in July of 2013. The state of Minnesota had been tracking her movements via radio collar since she became part of a long-term bear population ecology research study in 1981 when she was seven years old. At the time she had three female cubs in tow. Bear 56 spent the next 32 years peacefully being a bear, producing ten litters of cubs, the vast majority of which also defied the odds and lived to at least 14 months old. She successfully raised her last cub at age 25, and lived longer than any collared bear of any species studied in the world.

Less than five percent of wild bears live past their fifteenth birthday; about half die before they're five years old. She outlived by 16 years all 360 of her fellow radio-collared black bears in the study. "No known bears of any species have lived longer in the wild, based on age estimates from teeth taken from harvested bears," Dave Garshelis, the DNR's bear project leader, told the *Duluth News Tribune*.

Bear research biologist Karen Noyce, whose career began the same year Bear 56 was first collared, attributes the bear's long and healthy life to a good home range in a forested area with few people or major roads, a more shy and retiring nature than many bears which kept her away from homes and people, and plain old good luck.

Bear 56 near the end of her very long life. *© Karen Noyce*

In her last few years when her eyes were clouding, her hearing failed, and her teeth were showing excessive wear she got a little assistance from the state, which asked hunters not to shoot her if she crossed their path. In the two years before she died, she was more frequently seen foraging along trails and traveling dirt roads, likely because it was just easier on her old arthritic bones than traveling through the woods. "After following her all these years, I'm glad to know she died peacefully," said Noyce. "It was a fitting death for a fine old bear."

Home on the Range

Bears have loosely defined home ranges—the area where they forage for food, search for mates, and raise their young. The size of a bear's home range can vary from a mere square mile to more than 100 square miles. Ranges in the more open West are generally bigger than those in the East. Mature males mate with as many females as possible, so their home range is usually from 8 to 250 square miles, much larger than any one female's in the same area.

Females have smaller ranges than males, from one to 80 square miles. When juvenile females are ready to leave home they're often allowed to "move in next door," and share part of their mom's home range; most adolescent males are sent on their way and may have to travel 100 miles or more searching for food, shelter, and a home of their own.

Because bear ranges overlap, bears rely on a social hierarchy based on dominance to keep order, with smaller, more submissive bears going out of their way to avoid rubbing the top bears the wrong way. Although bears do wrestle, and jaw and spar much as dogs do, they seldom engage in serious fights, except in cases where mother bears are trying to protect their young from predatory adult males or two dominant males are fighting over a potential mate.

Why Do Bears Roam?

Most bears must routinely travel throughout their home range to find food, and daily circuits of 5 to 15 miles are not uncommon. But how far bears wander isn't always dictated by how much good food is available. Colorado bear biologist Tom Beck monitored two female cubs born the same year to different mothers with overlapping home ranges, so for the cubs, food availability and weather were pretty much the same. By the time the cubs were four years old, one had a range of 4 square miles; the other had a range of 15 square miles. Beck says there was no apparent biological or environmental reason for one bear to have a home range nearly four times as big as the other's. Perhaps some bears just have wanderlust.

Sizing Up Bears

People often swear that the bear involved in an unexpected encounter weighed 700 pounds and stood eight feet tall, a good indication of how things grow in our imaginations. Bulky builds and heavy fur coats make bears look bigger than they are. In one study, seasoned bear biologists overestimated the size of their subjects by as much as 25 percent. Little wonder wide-eyed hikers and rattled homeowners usually miss the mark.

From the tip of its highly sensitive nose to the end of its short stubby tail, an adult male black bear can measure 6 feet or more and stand 3½ feet high at the shoulder when standing on all four feet—about the height of your average four-year-old. A female is usually 4½ to 5 feet in length, and stands about 3 feet high at the shoulder.

National Park Service

A healthy adult black bear can weigh from under 100 pounds to more than 600 pounds. Bears, like humans, are sexually dimorphic, which means the males generally weigh more than the females. Depending on habitat and time of year, females weigh between 120 and 250 pounds, and pack on most of their bulk during their first three years of life. Males generally weigh between 180 and 300 pounds. If the eating is good, males will gain weight up until their tenth birthday, or sometimes beyond. Male black bears typically weigh about a third more than females in the same area.

The heaviest wild black bear on record is a male shot by a hunter in New Brunswick, Canada, in 1972 that weighed 902 pounds dressed; officials estimated its live weight at more than 1,000 pounds. Experts note that super-sized bears often have diets supplemented by human-provided food.

How big a bear grows depends both on its individual genetics and the quantity and quality of available food. Bears are almost always at their thinnest in late spring before green-up when they're still living off their winter fat reserves, and hit their high weights for the year just before denning in late fall.

A Fed Bear Is a Big Dead Bear

A bowhunter in Pennsylvania bagged an 879-pound bear in November 2012. It was soon discovered that "Bozo" had been dining off an artery-clogging diet of donuts, sweets, and other calorie-rich human foods since it was a cub some 17 years before. The 71-year old man who'd "raised" the bear considered it his pet, and was heartbroken when Bozo was killed. As was the hapless hunter, who got a lot of grief for taking a bear that had been trained to approach people for food.

It's against the law to feed bears in about half of the states and in the Canadian provinces of British Columbia and Alberta. Looking to humans for food puts both wildlife and people at risk. The people who create these problems might get fined, but the animal they've abused and taught to rely on them pays with its life.

© Tim Halvorson

What Color Is a Black Bear?

The black bear is a species, *Ursus americanus*, not a color. Black bears come in every color from the occasional snowy white and glacier blue to black as a moonless night, as well as every shade of blonde, brown and cinnamon. In the eastern third of North America, black bears are often black with brown muzzles; about one in four sport a jaunty white chest blaze. Head west and black bears are more likely to be brown-colored. In sun-drenched Arizona, 95 percent of black bears are some shade of brown. Researchers tracking individual black bears have documented cases of bears changing colors through the year, or from season to season. It's not unusual for a mother bear to give birth to cubs of several different colors. But blonde, brown or black, they're all still black bears.

Carnivore or Omnivore?

Scientifically, black bears are classified as carnivores, in the same category as dogs, cats, weasels and raccoons. But unlike other carnivores, the diet of the average black bear is less than 10 percent meat. And much of that comes from winter-killed deer, scavenged carcasses, and protein-packed insects.

Bears are often described as opportunistic feeders. Much like your average two-year-old child, a hungry black bear will eat or drink just about anything with calories, and some things without. Bears are hard-wired to spend the summer and fall gaining weight, and they adapt as best they can to whatever natural—and unnatural—foods are available every day.

The bulk of a bear's diet is nuts, berries, tender young grasses, and plants called leafy forbs, which are "anything green that isn't a grass or a tree." Bears will also scavenge any carcass they happen to come across and sometimes prey on young deer or elk. In some areas bears emerging from their dens in the spring expect to dine on winter-killed elk and deer while they wait for green-up; after a mild winter it can be tough to find enough early spring food.

Bears industriously turn over rocks and rip open logs in search of grubs, insects and fatty larvae, all important sources of protein. When bears dig through beehives they're looking for protein-packed developing bees as well as honey, Mother Nature's original energy food.

Some bears may occasionally prey on chickens, goats, sheep and young animals, particularly when pens are close to forest cover and easy to approach.

Bears have the longest and most massive skulls of all the carnivores, but not the flesh-cutting cheek teeth of most predators or the grinding molars and efficient stomachs of herbivores like elk and deer. So bears must eat a lot to get the nutrition they need, and prefer the tender, newly developing and most digestible parts of green plants.

Natural Disasters for Bears

Conflicts with bears go up in years when natural foods are in short supply. Droughts, insect infestations, fires, floods, and late spring and early fall freezes can all have a big impact on how much natural forage is available, and when. Even mild winters can wreak havoc, reducing winter-killed deer and elk, an important spring food for bears in many places. Not much you can do about nature's endless cycles of feast or famine, but you can take note and be extra-vigilant in years when the natural pickings are slim and bears are busily exploring all options.

Built for Strength and Endurance

Black bears may have the digestive system of a meat-eater, and the ability to run up to 35 mph over short distances, but they just don't have the feet for efficiently hunting and chasing down a meal.

Bears are built for strength, not speed, with thick limbs, huge shoulders and short backs and feet. Rather than tapering from hip to foot like a cat's, a bear's thick muscles stretch the entire length of the leg, making it easy to walk 15 miles a day, but hard to sprint for any distance.

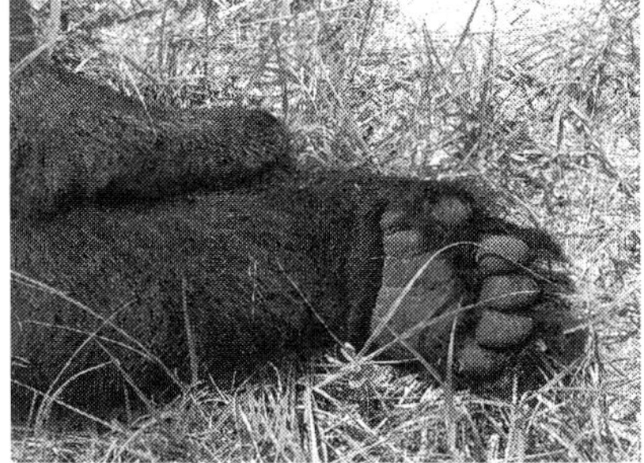

Black bears have short claws made for climbing, digging and ripping. *US Forest Service*

Bears have five toes on each foot, with non-retractable claws. A bear's hind footprint is eerily similar to a human footprint. That's because bears walk in plantigrade fashion, using their whole foot, heel to toe, much as we do, except bears generally walk on four feet instead of two.

Pure predators like the mountain lion are built to stalk and ambush speedy prey. Bears run like people instead of predators, so it's much harder for a black bear to chase down dinner.

Bears are incredibly strong, with jaws that can crunch through the bones of an adult deer, and powerful limbs that can rip a 10-inch log to shreds, dig out a winter den, or flip over 100-pound boulders searching for grubs. Even young bears are surprisingly strong; a six-month-old cub would win a wrestling match with most humans.

The Courtship of Bears

Bears typically mate in early and mid-summer, when dominant males roam through their expansive home ranges seeking out females in heat. I once watched a big, cinnamon-colored male lumber along at the heels of the object of his affection. Every once in a while she stopped and looked back over her shoulder; when he caught up, off she'd go

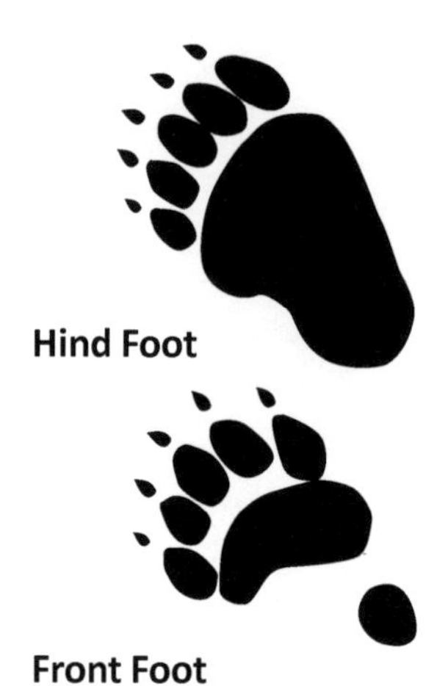

Bear claws are not retractable, but claw marks are not always visible in bear tracks.

again. I watched through my binoculars until they disappeared into the ponderosa pines, and can only assume he chased her until she was ready to be caught.

It's not uncommon to see bears traveling in pairs during mating season; the female is waiting until her biological clock tells her the timing is perfect. Once she finally gets the green light, the pair may stay together for a couple of days and mate several times. Females will mate with more than one male, and cubs from the same litter can have different fathers—a great way to keep the gene pool strong and healthy.

A Little Bit Pregnant

Unlike people, bears can be "a little bit pregnant." Because when it comes to having babies, Mother Nature has worked out a perfect plan for bears.

The physical demands of a summer pregnancy would be a real handicap to a female bear trying to fatten up before the winter. So even though bears mate in summer, the fertilized eggs, known as blastocysts, don't implant into the female's womb until sometime in the late fall when she weighs enough to sustain herself and her cubs for as long as six months without food. If she's underweight, sick or injured, the embryos are reabsorbed in order to give the mother bear the best chance of surviving to breed again.

If the bear is in good shape, the embryos implant and true development begins. Bears go through one of the shortest pregnancies on record for a mammal of their size, and in just about eight weeks, typically sometime in late January or early February, one to six cubs—usually two to three—are born, each about the size of a chipmunk.

The female rouses long enough to lick the cubs clean and consume

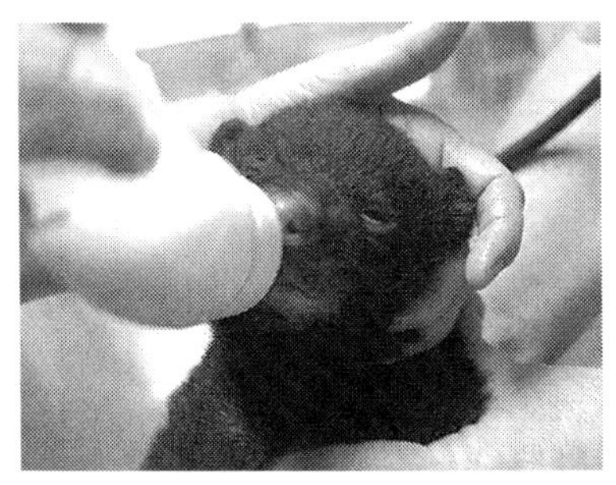
© Rich Beausoleil

the afterbirth, and then slips back into hibernation. There's no rest for the cubs; they must nurse and grow bigger and stronger before venturing out into the world in the spring.

A newborn bear looks like a pink, hairless rodent. It weighs less than a pound, and is a mere 1/300th to 1/500th the size of its mother. Compare that to the average human baby weighing in at 7½ pounds—already nearly five percent of the weight of a 150-pound adult.

A diet of rich mother's milk that's 33 percent fat ensures that cubs grow quickly. By the time they poke their curious noses into the world, they're three to four months old and weigh between four and eight pounds. Their bright blue eyes gradually change to brown as they grow older.

Compared to many mammals, black bears are slow reproducers; once a female reaches maturity, generally between age three and five, she can give birth to an average of two to three cubs every other year

Human mothers will recognize the look of long-suffering patience on this bear's face, and can surely sympathize with having so many hungry mouths to feed. *© Jenny E. Ross*

at most, depending on conditions and the mother's health, until her early to mid-twenties.

Older, more experienced bears tend to have larger litters than first-time moms; it's tough enough for an inexperienced mother to keep an eye on one or two rambunctious bundles of energy, never mind three or four.

Male black bears have nothing to do with rearing their offspring, and will sometimes kill the cubs of other males. The ever-vigilant female and her youngsters will be inseparable until the cubs are ready to strike out on their own, generally after their second winter.

The Annual Feeding Frenzy

From early spring until berries begin ripening in summer, an average-sized black bear will get by on about as many calories each day as a human of the same size—around 12 to 14 calories per pound of body weight. A 250-pound bear would need to eat about 3,000 calories a day just to maintain its body weight. Just like human moms, nursing bears need more calories.

Bears must add a thick layer of fat before turning in for the winter, so they're biologically programmed to "eat while the eating's good." The annual fall feeding frenzy is called hyperphagia.

When calorie-dense acorns and berries ripen and hibernation is looming, black bears become eating machines. During hyperphagia bears need to gain three to five pounds a day. That's 30,000 berries a day. To find that much food, bears forage up to 20 hours a day, routinely traveling outside their spring and summer ranges to seasonal feeding grounds where berries, acorns or other natural foods like spawning salmon are abundant.

Human-bear conflicts often go up in spring and early summer when available natural foods have fewer calories and in years with natural food failures. Bears determined to survive may resort to investigating human food sources. See the section "At Home in Bear Country" for tips on how to prevent problems for bears and people during food-stressed times.

Ontario Bear Wise reports that female bears with cubs are more likely to be killed in food-failure years, falling victim to landowners protecting property, hunters, agency removal, and accidents with cars and trains. This is most likely due to the fact that mother bears are working very hard to feed their offspring and venturing into places they might not normally go. Higher mortality for moms means that more cubs are orphaned during food-failure years.

A Long Winter's Nap

Bears don't den because it's cold; they put themselves to sleep for the winter because of dwindling food supplies. In far northern Minnesota and Canada, bears may spend six months in their dens. In milder climates like the Sierras, they might den from mid-December until March or early April. In southern latitudes where food is available all year, bears may den for shorter periods of time and sleep less deeply. In Florida only pregnant females den up for the winter; other bears may "nest" in dense vegetation for a few weeks or a month.

Bears make their dens in natural caves, hollow trees and logs, or shallow cavities they've dug out beneath tree roots. In some areas bears "nest" in a tree-hollow far above the ground or make a bed on the ground out of twigs and vegetation and patiently wait for Old Man Winter to cover them with an insulating blanket of snow. And most bear biologists have a tale or two about a bear that settled in for the winter beneath some unsuspecting homeowner's deck or porch. Bear dens are usually quite space-efficient to help conserve body heat, and remarkably clean and odor free, in stark contrast to bears' odoriferous nature the rest of the year.

Do Bears Really Hibernate?

A denning bear is a marvelous example of recycling at its best: it can go as many as 200 days without eating, drinking, or visiting the outhouse. Bears have a unique ability to reuse protein by-products and they lose fat, not muscle, while they live off the fat reserves they worked so hard to acquire. They also recycle calcium back into their bones, avoiding the bone loss that's typically caused by long periods of inactivity. If humans had the same ability, you wouldn't have to worry about holiday weight gain. You'd just go to sleep fat and happy in January, and wake up fit and trim in June.

Some scientists believe that bears don't actually hibernate, because hibernating mammals like bats, marmots, squirrels and rodents enter what is almost a state of suspended animation; their body temperatures drop drastically and metabolic processes slow nearly to a halt. True or "deep" hibernators must wake up every few days and reboot their metabolisms, drink some water, go to the bathroom, and nibble some stored food before sinking back into oblivion. But Yellowstone National Park's long-time bear biologist Kerry Gunther says that many scientists now consider bears super hibernators—able to hibernate for four to six months with few harmful side effects.

A bear's body temperature only drops about 12 degrees, and they don't eat, urinate or defecate. Respiration drops to just one breath every 45 seconds, compared to six to ten breaths a minute while bears are active. Heart rates drop by more than half, from 40–50 beats per minute to 8–19 during hibernation. Thanks to their big fur coats, body heat is lost slowly, which allows bears to cut their metabolic rate by 50 to 60 percent.

Bears often change position in the den, and may even wander out into the world for brief periods, then go back to sleep. Because bears don't have to warm up before they can move quickly, a denning bear can swiftly react to danger, so don't crawl into a bear den. Hibernating mother bears routinely nurse and even clean up after their cubs while they are "asleep," something any new human mother can easily relate to.

Researchers at the University of Alaska Fairbanks continuously monitoring five bears denning in artificial dens reported that the bears' metabolic rates dropped 35 percent more than the drop in body temperatures alone would account for, with metabolisms averaging an energy-saving 25 percent of the basic summer rate. The monitoring also revealed periods during denning when bears shivered their body

Lack of natural food sources is what sends bears into their winter dens.

temperatures up several degrees. Most studies show that metabolic rates don't drop significantly. The researchers speculate that may be because most studies rely on random samples while their study provided continuous monitoring. In the Alaska study, heartbeats also fell from 55 beats per minute to 14 erratic beats, which could also save energy. The team discovered it was several weeks after bears emerged from their dens in the spring before metabolic rates returned to normal, which could be a means of conserving energy while natural foods consist mostly of tender spring vegetation and winter-killed animals.

Priceless Secrets of Hibernation

Even though bears don't eat, drink or go to the bathroom while they are hibernating and their body temperature and heart rate drops dramatically, black bears somehow manage to put their enforced rest to good use, healing injuries without infection and little scarring, according to the journal *Integrative Zoology*. There's hope that someday researchers may be able to create pharmaceuticals for humans that could induce a type of hibernation which would allow traumatic muscle and bone injuries to heal better.

And if bears could sell the secret to sleeping away fat without losing any muscle, they would become instant bear billionaires. Scientists interested in discovering ways to aid human weight loss are trying to unlock this particular biochemical mystery.

Spring Wake-Up Call

When temperatures warm up and food is available once again, bears leave their dens. Adult males are generally the first bears out and prowling around; subadults of both sexes, females with yearlings, and solitary adult females come out next. Moms with newborn cubs are normally the last to emerge, and often remain near their dens for several more weeks. After bears wake up they finally heed the call of nature, and then go in search of a good drink, and eventually a few mouthfuls of something tender and green.

A Nose for Food

"A cookie crumb fell in the woods. The eagle saw it. The deer heard it. The bear smelled it, and went looking for the rest of the box." That's not exactly how the old Native American proverb goes, but it does highlight a bear's single most powerful sense: its nose.

Think you have a pretty good sense of smell? Imagine being able to stand on your porch and smell the enticing aroma of chicken grilling five miles away. A bear's nasal mucosa area is 100 times larger than yours, making a bear's nose seven times more sensitive than a bloodhound's famed sniffer. Bear biologist Gary Brown reported that a black bear in California was observed traveling upwind three miles in a straight line, unerringly following its nose to the carcass of a dead deer.

Bears can detect molecules of food so small they're invisible to the naked eye, sniff out a candy bar stuffed under a car seat from outside the car, and tell the difference between people and animals from trace scents left in footprints.

So is it any wonder that the leftovers from yesterday's dinner decomposing in the trash send out tempting odors a hungry bear finds easy to follow...and hard to ignore?

All Ears

It's pretty hard to administer a hearing test to a conscious black bear, but scientists believe that bears hear in the ultrasonic range of 16–20 kilohertz or higher—much better than humans do. Bears have been observed responding to the click of a camera shutter more than 50 yards away. And to a foraging grizzly bear, the noise made by ground squirrels, mice, and voles underground must be as loud as a dinner bell, as grizzlies are often seen digging rodents out of their tunnels.

A bear's ears are a good clue to a bear's age. Ears don't grow, so the bigger they look, the younger the bear. *© Tom Beck*

Do Bears Need Glasses?

It was once thought that bears were color blind and had poor vision, but studies show that bears can see about as well as we do, although there is evidence they are a bit nearsighted, which could actually help them locate berries, grubs and other small delicacies. Bears have good depth perception and distance vision, and can recognize forms over a hundred yards away. They also see in color, which could help with food identification. Watch a bear delicately stripping berries from a branch or licking up ants scurrying out of an anthill, and you'll have no doubt a bear can see what it's doing.

Smarter Than the Smartest Dog

Yogi Bear has a famous line: "Hey, Boo Boo, I'm smarter than your average bear." That would make Yogi an ursine Einstein, because your average bear is pretty darn smart.

Bear biologists who've measured bears' intelligence report that the average black bear is significantly smarter than a German shepherd, widely regarded as the smartest dog, and put bears' intelligence somewhere between dogs and primates. Bears have the heaviest brains, relative to body length, of any carnivore.

Being super-smart helps bears discover food, identify and avoid danger, find mates, and allows mother bears to teach their young everything they've learned. But watch a bear play "slide down the snow bank," or "tree teeter-totter," and it's hard not to believe that sometimes bears just wanna have fun.

Can Bears Reason?

There's plenty of evidence that bears can recognize a wide variety of objects, from beehives and berry bushes to coolers, refrigerators and campers. Bears also have a remarkable ability to learn and generalize to a simple concept level.

So if a bear discovers a bird feeder in one backyard and nothing bad happens when it bats it down and gobbles up the birdseed, it will check out other yards hoping to find more bounty. If it does, the bear "reasons" that this must be a place with a good crop of "bear-feeders," and keeps looking. And since it found a good meal once, it's likely to come back for more.

A recent study involving bear siblings from a zoo in Michigan used rugged touch-screen computers to reward bears with food treats for correctly identifying and sorting images. At least one of the bears learned to distinguish animals from objects like landscapes and cars, but couldn't quite separate bears from people—perhaps adding credence to the theory that bears view us as a sort of "uber-bear," and treat us accordingly.

Good Memories

A bear's ability to quickly learn and retain information helps it keep a mental catalogue of all the food sources in its home range, and know when they're usually available. Mother bears patiently teach their cubs where to find food, from the earliest spring grasses to the acorns and berries that ripen in the fall. An animal that can remember buffalo berries ripen the second week in August on the south slope and the third week on the north slope has no trouble noting that every Thursday night the community dumpster is full of tasty trash. Bears will return unerringly day after day or year after year to a place that has provided life-sustaining food, whether it's a berry patch or a garbage dump.

Curious and Resourceful

Bears are not fussy eaters. For a bear, a spirit of culinary adventure is a necessary survival trait. You never know when a late spring freeze, summer drought, or human development is going to make a particular food source dry up. That's why bears are genetically programmed to investigate everything and anything that might possibly be nourishing. That curiosity and resourcefulness can help keep a bear alive. Or lead it to dangerous new food sources like garbage, bird feeders, or backyard chicken coops.

Shy and Evasive

Centuries ago when grizzly bears roamed over much of North America, black bears learned to share space with their more powerful cousins by avoiding confrontations at all costs. They took to the forest where there were plenty of trees to climb and places to hide, and avoided the open plains where they'd have to stand and defend themselves.

Under most circumstances a wild black bear that detects a human nearby will do its best to avoid an encounter. But bears are also nervous and easily frightened, especially when confronted by the unfamiliar. Surprising, cornering or approaching a bear can trigger a flight or fight response. If flight isn't possible, the bear may respond by fighting back. See the section "Crossing Paths with Bears" for detailed information.

Remarkably Tolerant

Even under the most trying of circumstances, black bears are remarkably tolerant of people. Steve Herrero tells a tale that demonstrates both the tolerance of bears and the cruelty of some humans. He once watched three teenagers chase two cubs up a tree, pelting them with rocks while the mother bear watched. Eventually the sow climbed up and tried to shield her cubs with her body. At that point Steve the dispassionate scientist gave way to Steve the protector of nature; the boys threatened him with a tire iron, but he stood his ground. Apparently they were willing to take on a bear, but not an outraged bear scientist. Steve notes if they'd harassed grizzly bear cubs, they would almost certainly have been injured or killed.

All-Around Animal Athletes

Bears may not be built for long-distance marathons, but they can run up to 35 mph for short distances, and despite the common myth, have no trouble running downhill, uphill or across the hill. Olympic gold medalist Usain Bolt could theoretically run more than 27 mph, but the average human is lucky to manage a third of that. Bears are also good swimmers and even adult black bears are great tree climbers. You can't outrun, out swim, or out climb a bear. ❖

Most bears seem to enjoy the water, wading, splashing, soaking, floating and swimming with ease. Bears take to the water to play, cool off, and hunt for food.

The Last Black Bear in Florida

I could easily be typing those depressing "remember when" words today. But instead I get to tell you a remarkable story of loss and recovery.

A century ago as many as 10,000 black bears roamed throughout most of Florida, thriving in a climate that produced a year-round Garden of Eden of natural foods, denning sites, and dense cover. But by the 1960s decades of unregulated and illegal hunting and a human invasion that gobbled up habitat faster than you can say "Sunshine State" had decimated the bear population.

In 1974 when the bear was first listed as Threatened, human encroachment with networks of roads and rapid development had

Florida Fish & Wildlife Conservation Commission

all conspired to isolate Florida's bear populations, resulting in some areas with as few as 20 bears. All told, just 300 bears were stubbornly trying to survive on eight "islands" of mostly public lands. Back then Florida was home to 6.8 million people.

Today the black bear population numbers around 3,000. And after nearly four decades of hard work, in 2012 Florida's unique black bear subspecies, *Ursus americanus floridanus*, was declared healthy and stable enough to be removed from the state's list of Threatened Species.

Restoring the bear population to health was a long, complex and evolutionary process that involved many disciplines from the field of wildlife management as well as a public whose wants and needs were much more divergent than the needs of bears.

Hunting regulations were overhauled to reduce the number of female bears taken. Hunting was eliminated everywhere bear populations were unstable, and then closed statewide in 1994. Land acquisition programs were developed, including the Florida Forever program which has acquired more than 2.4 million acres of conservation lands. The Florida Fish and Wildlife Conservation Commission (FWC) and federal agencies worked together with private landowners to improve habitat on their land through easements and incentive programs.

Surveys showed that Floridians valued their black bears, but there wasn't enough public awareness or understanding of what was needed to ensure bears remained a viable part of the Florida landscape. In 1993 only 67 percent of Floridians were aware that black bears even existed in the state.

Wide-ranging public education programs, including an innovative elementary school curriculum built around bears, set out to tackle that problem. By 2008 awareness of bears had risen by more than 25 percent and 93 percent of people agreed that Florida black bears should be protected so future generations will see them. An overwhelming percentage (91 percent) of Florida folks also believed that wildlife education was important and 89 percent enjoyed learning about wildlife.

Florida Fish & Wildlife Conservation Commission

Of course social research has clearly proven that short-term awareness does not necessarily translate into long-term sustainable action, something illustrated all too well by the fact that bear complaints grew from one in 1978 to more than 6,000 in 2013.

One of the plan's goals is to reduce complaints by two-thirds, and not just so FWC can spend less time responding to bear calls. Research shows that negative publicity can make people less tolerant of bears.

With nearly 20 million residents, Florida is now the third most populated state. Add in an astonishing 80 million tourists each year and you get an idea of the monumental job of reaching the right people with the right messages and persuading them to do the right things.

To achieve long-term changes in lifestyles, education has to go beyond awareness and understanding to focus on practical ways to coexist, prevent and solve problems, and create opportunities for individuals and groups to get involved and take ownership. The public needs to embrace being bear-smart, and frown on being bear-stupid.

A 215-page Bear Management Plan that took five years of research, thousands of hours of work, and ongoing input from all the key stakeholders was adopted in 2012. The plan lays out four main objectives and multiple courses of action to ensure that the future of Florida's bears will never again be in doubt.

It's an ambitious plan with goals that range from creating continuous habitat corridors for bears to establishing official Bear Smart Communities using British Columbia's (with the province's enthusiastic support) stringent requirements and protocols.

Realizing that ownership and involvement in the process was the only way to create an action plan that would work in the real world, FWC identified several key audiences: communities, private landowners, governmental, nongovernmental and business organizations, and FWC staff, because staff understanding and buy-in would be critical to long-term success.

Florida's bears could have become a footnote in the natural history books. Instead it was a proud day for all the groups that had worked so hard to restore the bears—and for the people of Florida—when the plan was passed in 2012 and bears were officially removed from the Threatened Species list.

Defenders of Wildlife initiated their Habitat for Bears campaign in 1994, and has been working with FWC ever since on long-term plans for managing and connecting bear habitat throughout the state.

Their press release echoed the sentiment expressed by the authors of the plan. "While delisting is a marker of success, the species still needs careful stewardship to ensure that it keeps thriving...continued conservation measures are also needed to ensure the smaller bear subpopulations grow to sustainable size. The Florida black bear still has a ways to go before we can say that its recovery is complete, but the delisting is a great sign that this species is on its way. Defenders of Wildlife is proud to have made a significant contribution to the recovery effort for this special bear."

Florida's Four Main Objectives:

1) Maintain a sustainable statewide bear population, and ensure that the smaller subpopulations are increased to a minimum of 200 bears each.

2) Maintain habitat in sufficient quantity, quality and connectivity to meet the population objection; increase connectivity between habitat areas.

3) Reduce human-bear conflicts by coordinating with local government officials in primary bear range to implement methods for reducing conflicts; revise bear policies to create a comprehensive approach to conflict management; develop protocols to capture knowledge, standardize response and improve effectiveness;

and create partnerships that will help FWC resolve human-bear conflicts.

4) Help Florida citizens have a better understanding of bears, support bear conservation measures and contribute to reducing conflicts through education and outreach programs; partnerships with government, NGOs (see the glossary in the appendix) and other stakeholders; and develop Bear Smart Communities in areas of high bear activity.

If you've never read a bear management plan, search the website of your state or province's wildlife management agency. Most of the plans are hundreds of pages long and contain a wealth of information and resources.

Few people realize that public opinion and input plays an important role in crafting and implementing these plans that guide the future of the species. I was proud to be a consultant for Virginia's enlightened new 10-year bear management plan. ❖

© Cyndi Hoxie

4

Grizzly Bears in Brief

Back when Lewis and Clark first explored the West in the early 1800s an estimated 50,000 grizzly bears *(Ursus arctos)* roamed from Alaska to central Mexico and from California to the Great Plains, sharing vast expanses of open land with the Native Americans. Native populations respected and even revered the great bear. The tide of European settlers was not as tolerant, and grizzly bears were shot on sight, poisoned, and trapped in an effort to eradicate them.

Grizzly bears are slow to reproduce and slow to raise their cubs; the wholesale slaughter caused populations to plummet. By the 1930s small remnant populations of grizzly bears survived in less than two percent of their historic range.

This isn't a fight; these grizzly bears are just horsing around. *© Deb Cheuvront*

The U.S. Fish and Wildlife Service realized that without intervention and protection one of the most magnificent mammals on the planet faced extinction in the lower 48 states. In 1975 they listed the grizzly bear as a threatened species under the Endangered Species Act.

Grizzly Bear Range Outside of Alaska
Small populations of grizzly bears occupy small pockets of land in the lower 48 states; greater numbers are found in parts of Alaska and Canada.

Today public attitudes have changed from persecution to preservation, and grizzly bears are recovering. Between 629 and 740 grizzly bears live in the Greater Yellowstone ecosystem, with another 1,000 or so in the Northern Continental Divide. Very small populations also survive in northern Idaho, western Montana, and the North Cascades in upper Washington State. About 30,000 grizzly/brown bears live in Alaska and another 20,000 to 25,000 inhabit Canada, with more than half of the Canadian bears found in British Columbia and the Northwest Territories. Populations in Alaska and Canada are strong and healthy enough for the great bears to be classified and managed as a big game species.

Research shows the population in the Greater Yellowstone ecosystem is strong, and the area may have reached its actual carrying capacity—the number of bears that can make a living there. It's possible that grizzlies living in and around Yellowstone National Park and the Northern Continental Divide could soon come off the Endangered Species list. Management and future preservation of the species would then be shared by the federal government and the states of Montana, Wyoming and Idaho.

Strong opinions exist about whether grizzlies should be delisted, but in late 2013 the members of the Interagency Grizzly Bear Committee voted unanimously to end federal protection. Dr. Chris

Servheen, who has led the recovery team since its inception in 1983, says that "If we don't delist when the bears are recovered, public and political support will evaporate. We have to signal a touchdown has been made."

Grizzly Bear or Brown Bear?

Is it a brown bear or a grizzly bear? What's the difference? In some ways, that depends on where you live. In Europe and Asia they're called brown bears. But in North America typically only the bears that live along the coast of Alaska and Canada are referred to as brown bears. These bears tend to be larger and more tolerant of each other because there's plenty to eat, including salmon and whale carcasses. The smaller—smaller being a somewhat relative term—bears that live inland and in the lower 48 are called grizzlies. In this handbook, the term grizzly refers to all members of *Ursus arctos*.

The Grizzly Basics

The common name grizzly comes from "grizzled," which means hair flecked with gray at the ends or a mixture of grey and dark colors—that's where "silvertip" came from. A grizzly bear's coat can range from pale blond to many shades of brown or occasionally red or black.

Grizzly bears need a lot of open space—their home ranges are typically much larger than a black bear's home range. Males can roam over 200 to 500 square miles, so ranges typically overlap with other bears. Females have smaller home ranges, averaging 50 to 300 square miles, but that's still a lot of room to roam.

As true omnivores, grizzlies will eat just about anything with calories, including berries, roots, bulbs, nuts, and cutworm moths. And in the summer grizzlies dig ground-dwelling rodents out of the high-elevation boulder fields by the hundreds of thousands.

Grizzlies typically eat more meat than black bears, and will hunt moose, elk, mountain goats, and mountain sheep; they'll also feast on carrion. You've probably seen television coverage of enterprising coastal grizzlies fishing the spawning salmon out of the streams in the late summer. In fact, coastal grizzlies eat so well on their diet of fat- and protein-rich salmon that they grow much larger than their inland cousins, and the coast can support as many as 40 percent more bears than the inland habitat.

Grizzly bears stand about 3½ feet tall when on all fours; they can be 5 to 7 feet tall when standing on their hind legs. Grizzlies are dimorphic, which means that male bears are much larger than females, often weighing twice as much. Bears on the Kodiak archipelago are even larger; a mature male can be 10 feet tall standing up.

Grizzly bears don't breed until they're at least five years old, and cubs stay with their moms between two and four years; black bear cubs typically go out on their own in their second summer. So even with a lifespan in the wild of 20 to 25 years, a female grizzly bear typically raises far fewer cubs than a mother black bear.

One of the single biggest threats to grizzly bears is loss of habitat and the resulting loss of food sources. Shrinking habitat also pushes

© Deb Cheuvront

grizzly bears closer to human developments, where their keen noses often lead them to the same food sources that get black bears in trouble: garbage, bird feeders, pet and livestock feed, as well as things like backyard chicken coops.

Their long front claws are excellent for digging roots—and prying open garbage containers and freezers. Their massive shoulders and incredible strength are handy for moving boulders in search of insects—and ripping open a shed full of feed. Their keen sense of smell can lead them to a carcass or a ripe patch of berries miles away—and to an overflowing dumpster. They are well-equipped for hunting large animals, which became evident when mountain pine beetles devastated white bark pine trees, almost eliminating an important food source for grizzlies in the Yellowstone ecosystem. The great bears adapted by eating more berries and dining on more elk, moose and bison.

Living and Playing in Grizzly Country

Grizzly bears are smart, persistent, curious, clever, and incredibly strong. Female grizzlies are excellent and patient mothers, spending up to four years teaching their offspring how to survive on their own. Unlike black bears, they are very protective of their young and will defend them from real or perceived danger at almost any cost.

Grizzlies are attracted to people by the same things that attract black bears: easy-to-get-at calories.

Living and playing in grizzly country is a privilege that carries with it an enormous responsibility to do so safely and without causing problems for bears.

Most serious grizzly bear injuries result from people being in the wrong place at the wrong time...surprising a bear at close range, or coming between a bear and a food source or a protective mother grizzly and her cubs.

Recreating in Grizzly Country

While many of the guidelines are the same, there are some important differences between how black bears and grizzlies relate and react to humans. If you're hiking in grizzly country, you need to know the latest directives and local conditions before you hit the trail. Never ignore closures, restrictions, and other warnings; there's a very good reason why they are in place. Travel in groups of two or more, and make sure everyone has bear spray, and knows how to use it.

If you're on a trail that suddenly narrows so much you need to crawl through, you are probably on a bear trail, not a people trail. These grizzly "mazes" are common in grizzly country. Leave the maze to the bears, and hike someplace else.

Grizzly bears seldom attack unprovoked, but can be aggravated by behavior that most black bears suffer without retaliating. Most grizzly attacks result from sudden surprise encounters. Getting between a mother grizzly and her cubs or startling a bear protecting a carcass can quickly trigger a defensive response. Even a quick swipe of a massive paw meant to tell you to go away can send you to the emergency room. Make noise from time to time; hiking, running or cycling silently through dense cover is asking for trouble.

A gut pile or mound of twigs and leaves with various animal parts peeking out is a sign you should leave the area immediately, and remain on high alert. It's a myth that grizzlies cannot climb trees, but with their long curved claws designed for digging they are not as agile as black bears. As with black bears, running triggers a chase response and the bear will likely reach you before you reach the tree. But if you are in imminent danger climbing up as high as you can may be your best option.

Grizzlies are also very protective of their personal space; you need to stay at least 100 yards away unless you are on a guided viewing tour or in an enclosed vehicle. It's neither safe nor smart to try to creep up for a better look or a better picture. More than one photographer's final close-up photo has been of a charging grizzly.

How can you tell a grizzly bear from a black bear?

Size and color can be confusing, as many black bears are brown, and a large black bear can easily be the size of a small grizzly. Take a good look at these illustrations and you'll see there are several points of difference between the two species. ❖

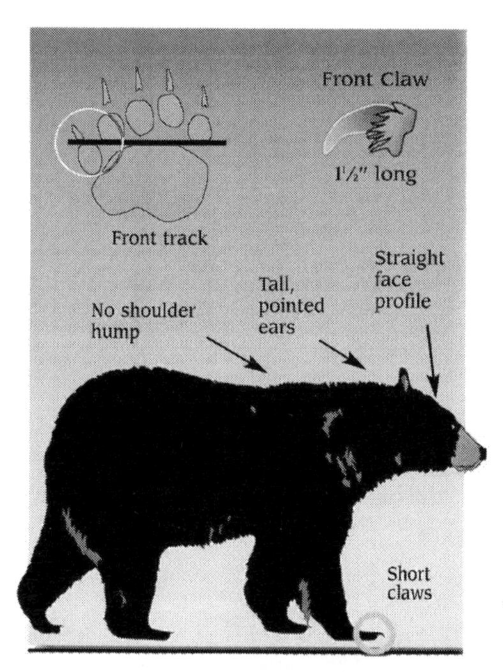

Black Bear

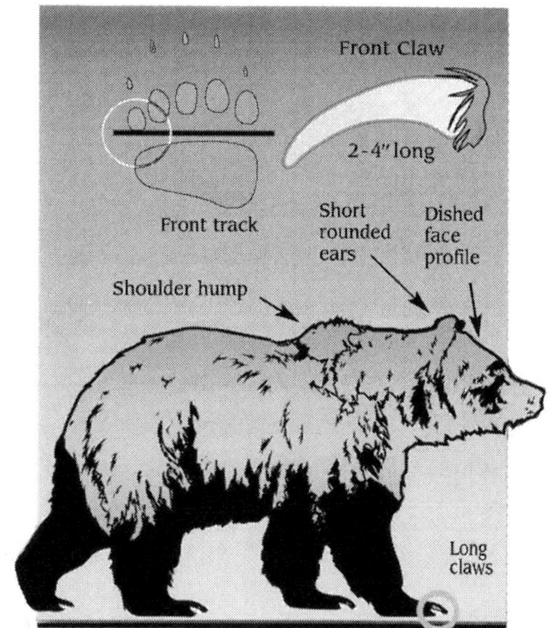

Grizzly Bear

Courtesy of Chuck Bartlebaugh, Be Bear Aware

The Great Kodiak Bear

Arguably the largest bears in the world belong to a subspecies which has lived in isolation on the Kodiak Archipelago off the southeastern coast of Alaska for about 12,000 years: *Ursus arctos middendorffi*, popularly known as the Kodiak bear.

A large male can stand more than 10 feet tall on its hind legs and weigh up to 1,200 pounds. Female Kodiak bears are about 30 percent lighter and 20 percent smaller than males. Like all bears they are generally solitary, but if there's a concentrated food source like a whale carcass or salmon-spawning stream, they will congregate in large groups.

The eating on the Kodiak Archipelago is so good that despite their impressive size, Kodiak bears have some of the smallest home ranges of any brown bears. In order to cope with all that enforced togetherness they've developed an especially complex language of vocalizations and body postures to express their feelings and minimize fighting.

The original human inhabitants of Kodiak were the Alutiiq people, a seafaring coastal culture which shared rich salmon-spawning streams and beaches with abundant brown bears. Alutiiqs considered "Tacuka'aq" a powerful spirit who was a liaison between the spirit world and their world.

© Larry Van Daele, Alaska Department of Fish & Game

Through understanding and mutual respect, bears and people coexisted with few problems for thousands of years.

Other human-bear relations have not always been peaceful on Kodiak. Bears and cattle ranchers had been at odds since the 1800s. Kodiak bears were commercially hunted until 1925, even though their enormous pelts were only worth about ten bucks. Most bear conflicts with ranchers and other residents have been resolved, and with only a few exceptions, bears and people are once again peacefully coexisting.

Today, about 13,000 Kodiak residents share space with a flourishing population of 3,500 bears. That's a bear density of about 0.7 bears per square mile, or about one bear for every four humans. Despite the high human-to-bear ratio, in the past 90 years there's been just one human fatality.

Managing Bears, Motivating People

5

A Look at Bear Management

Bear biologist, game warden, wildlife agent, conflict specialist, bear manager. The lexicon of terms that have developed over the years to describe people whose jobs include studying and working with wildlife populations as well as dealing with human/wildlife conflicts can be confusing. Some people think that bear managers actually manage bears much like a boss manages employees. So, of course, people think it's the manager's job to "come get their bear" or otherwise solve any problems they might be having. Even when it's the people who are causing the problems.

I've talked with hundreds of bear biologists, wildlife officers and

© Tom Beck

A collared 9-year-old research bear being released in Nevada. *© John Humphreys*

researchers all over North America and I don't think I've met a single one who went to school for 18 or 20 years because they had a burning desire to give PowerPoint presentations on why people need to lock up their garbage. Many of them would much rather face a cranky bear than a room full of homeowners. Or study steaming piles of bear scat instead of shoveling through mountains of the human variety.

They do have a burning desire to leave the natural world better than they found it. They want to find better ways to manage wildlife populations and habitats in the face of ever increasing human encroachment. They want to make a difference.

Bears have no clue anyone is responsible for managing them. They're managed by their basic drives: food, shelter, safety, propagation of the species, self-preservation. Bears are masters at acting in their own self-interest. And it's pretty tough to convince a hungry bear that diving into a dumpster full of food is a bad idea. Especially when a few minutes of exploration is rewarded with a truckload of calories that will ensure another week of survival.

The human component of bear management has two sides: reactive (dealing with problems and conflicts with specific bears as they occur) and proactive (trying to prevent more conflicts with all bears from occurring.)

Dealing with "one bear at a time" involves resolving an immediate problem in a specific area with a particular bear or bears. Managers use a variety of tactics you'll learn more about later in this section. This approach to problem-solving often ends up on the nightly news, with bears being chased, harassed, trapped, or otherwise discouraged from hanging around people-places. Sometimes there's a happy ending for the bear. Sometimes there isn't. But no matter what happens, dealing with one bear at a time can never solve the real problem. It's like sticking a Band-Aid on a big open wound that really needs to be cleaned out, stitched up, and dosed with antibiotics.

No one wants to kill bears for being in the wrong place at the wrong time and doing what their human neighbors consider the wrong thing. In wildlife management, killing an animal that's involved in a conflict situation that's not threatening human safety is a last resort. Removing one bear doesn't get to the root of the problem, because unless humans change their behavior, another bear will take its place at the all-you-can-paw-through buffet. So management agencies have developed a whole range of approaches aimed at teaching people why the problem occurred in the first place, persuading them to remove attractants, and encouraging the bear to abandon its behavior. ❖

Bears should never feel at home around your home. Teaching them to avoid human places can prevent problems for people and bears. *© Paul Conrad*

6

Relocation: "Come Get Your Bear"

When people are frightened, anxious, or nervous about bears, they want "someone" to make their problem go away. Tell them the bear will be relocated, and they heave a sigh of relief. Their problem gets trapped, tranquilized, ear-tagged and tattooed, loaded onto a transport truck and hauled off. They imagine the bear living happily ever after out in the sanitized Disney version of the woods "where it belongs." They feel good because they didn't want the bear to die because of something they did. But all too often, sooner or later that's exactly what happens.

When a bear is relocated (moved outside its home range) or translocated (moved within its home range), if whatever attracted it in the first place isn't eliminated, the void created will be quickly filled by another bear in search of an easy meal. The end result is a never-ending conveyor belt of bears, problems and temporary solutions.

Why Relocations Usually Fail

It seems like a great idea. Trap the bear. Move it somewhere there aren't any people. Give it a second chance. Solve the problem. Write a happy ending for both people and bear. While it can work with bears that are not yet human food-conditioned, study after study shows that in most cases relocating bears just isn't effective.

Today there are precious few places in bear country where there are no people. And most of those precious places with no people and good habitat are already home to plenty of bears.

It's hard work being a bear. Years of trial, error and exploration go into identifying every possible source of food, water, shelter, and danger. A strange bear in a strange land can literally starve to death if it doesn't know where to find food. Relocated bears can have bear problems of their own if the resident bruins react badly to having a new competitor for food, denning space, and mates dropped into their turf. A relocated bear might even be killed by a dominant bear already occupying the area.

Years with high numbers of human-bear conflicts are often also years with natural food shortages—times when a late spring freeze, a hot, dry summer, or a natural disaster causes widespread failures of natural food sources like berries or nuts. A bear moved from one food-short area to another is at a double disadvantage. It's unfamiliar with the new territory, and there's not much food to be had.

Bears are creatures of habit. When bears are moved, their behavior patterns move with them. Bears that have already learned to rely on human food sources often pick up where they left off and end up in conflicts with people in their new territories. When a tagged bear goes back to its old habits, chances are it won't get a third chance. When there's a risk of further problems and interactions, public safety always comes first. Some hapless wildlife manager in the bear's new "home" will probably have to kill it.

Florida Fish & Wildlife Conservation Commission

Bears have highly developed homing instincts. And they don't know home is no longer a safe place to be. So most relocated bears try to find their way back. Bears have crossed desert basins and mountain ranges, dodged cars (sometimes successfully) on four-lane highways, and traveled more than a hundred miles to return home. Once they are back in familiar territory, they're prone to resuming the activities that got them moved in the first place. And that often gets them killed.

Most wildlife managers know moving human food-conditioned bears is not likely to be an effective long-term solution. Overall statistics are pretty grim, with the majority of relocations failing—from the bear's point of view—for one reason or another.

Yosemite National Park made a total of 124 relocations between 1989 and 1993. Bears must be relocated within park boundaries, which limited the distance they could be moved. Approximately 80 percent of the relocations failed, with the bears eventually resuming their problem behavior and being recaptured in developed areas in the years following their release. After numerous research studies, Yosemite and sister parks Kings Canyon and Sequoia have, except in unusual circumstances, stopped relocating bears.

In British Columbia, they've given up on relocating black bears. The British Columbia Ministry of the Environment studied the issue and decided that the low success rate combined with the high cost in dollars and time made it impractical to move black bears any distance. So each year somewhere between 500 and 1,000 black bears and as many as 100 grizzly bears lose their lives as a direct result of conflicts between people and bears.

When Relocation Can Work

Relocation has been used successfully to reintroduce bears into an area where the resident population had been wiped out. For conflict resolution, the best odds of long-term success are with bears that are not already human-food conditioned. For practical purposes, this means they have to be trapped and moved while they are on the first few rungs of the behavioral progression ladder (see Chapter 1). Juvenile male bears are elbowed out of their home range by their moms sometime during their second summer and are already looking for somewhere to call home. So if they can be moved to suitable habitat where they don't have to compete with dominant males, there may be a better chance they'll adapt and stay put.

Learning to Navigate

Much has been written about black bears' uncanny ability to unerringly return to their home range despite being moved long distances in hopes of preventing further problems. A study in Ontario showed that homing ability may be learned, rather than inherent: 81 percent of adult bears homed successfully, but only 23 percent of juveniles. And juvenile bears were not able to return home from as far away as adults. The study speculates homing ability may be dependent on the bear's age and how well established its home range is.

Your Opinion Counts

Agencies set management policies, but public opinion influences that process and is much more important than the public realizes. When people make it known they don't want bears moved or destroyed except as a last resort and are willing to do their part to make that happen, it's easier for managers to go to bat for bears, address the root causes of the problem, and get the funding they need to try other approaches. ❖

7

Other Non-Lethal Tactics

Aversive Conditioning

The aversive conditioning concept is based on a simple principle: if bears are smart enough to learn from positive experiences, they must be smart enough to learn from negative ones as well.

When a bear raids a garbage can, makes off with a bird feeder, or dives into a dumpster and comes up with a bag full of calorie-laden leftovers, and nothing bad happens, it learns that human places are safe, easy and rewarding places to forage.

Aversive conditioning is designed to teach the bear to associate people with danger, stop the behavior, leave the area, and avoid it in the future. The tactics are based on the principle that people can communicate with bears in a language that bears understand—body language. Fighting is not a commonly accepted way to solve problems in black bear society. In fact, a bear in the wild will do just about anything to avoid getting into paw-to-paw combat with another bear—especially one it thinks could kick its butt. That's why people employing aversive conditioning need to act with authority and confidence.

© Sara Tuttle

Tactics include everything from loud noises, hand-clapping and yelling to pelting the bear with beanbag rounds to giving chase with highly trained Karelian Bear Dogs. Unless you've been trained by your wildlife agency, don't try anything beyond yelling and hand-clapping on your own. You could get hurt, and bears can be seriously injured by supposedly non-lethal projectiles like rubber buckshot.

To be effective, aversive conditioning needs to be administered quickly and consistently, which can be pretty time-consuming if you're the bear biologist hiding in the bushes waiting for the bear to come back and make another run at somebody's bird feeder.

Bears are very smart, but they learn their lessons one bear at a time. There are no town meetings. Nobody tweets out reminders to stay away from human places or else. Mother bears pass on their knowledge to their cubs, and one day the female cubs that grow up will pass along those lessons to their own offspring. So trying to reeducate a bear that's learned humans provide good sources of food is a time-consuming, challenging and difficult job.

Aversive conditioning can drive bears away from problem areas long enough for people to fix the problems, but it's seldom effective if the root causes of the problems aren't addressed.

"Bears do not understand English or French, but they do understand a language of dominance and submission. By posturing or faking the bear into believing the human is in control of the situation, the wildlife manager can assert his dominance, and become the alpha bear—the one calling the shots," says Sylvia Dolson, executive director of Whistler's Get Bear Smart Society, and author of the *Non-Lethal Black Bear Management Guidebook*.

Capture and On-Site Release

Releasing a bear at the site of the problem is a technique that many bear experts and bear biologists feel is one of the most promising tools for reeducating bears. Typically the bear is trapped and given a complete physical. Sometimes a tooth is pulled to help determine the age of the bear, and the bear often gets a lip tattoo, ear tag, microchip, or radio collar for tracking. Eventually the bear is returned to the trap and allowed to recover completely from the anesthesia, which may take as long as overnight. It's important for the bear to be alert and fully conscious before it's released.

When the bear flees from the trap, it's yelled at, pelted with bean bag rounds, chased by trained bear dogs, or otherwise made miserable until it is well away from the release site and back somewhere suitable for the bear to be. At that point all harassment instantly stops: the bear is rewarded for heading back into the forest and it learns where the boundaries are.

This is referred to as hard on-site release to distinguish it from just opening the trap and allowing the bear to run off. It's considered a very effective form of hazing that can teach a bear to associate the capture/release site with a very bad experience it has no desire to repeat.

Several studies have shown that on-site release is an effective technique for getting bears to stop their behavior, with a much higher success rate than relocation.

"Relocating a bear is at best a tactic to buy time to remove attractants. This is not to be confused with on-site releases, which constitute the most effective bear-shepherding tool we've got—you catch a bear where it is getting into trouble, hold it a while, then set up the trap so the bear can get to cover quickly—but will also know exactly where it is. Having this chance to associate this experience with the place can teach a bear, in one go-round, that this is a place to avoid. You can't get those immediate results most of the time with other methods. It's basically saying to the bear...*See this? This is wrong. See those trees? You go to those trees and stay out of here and we leave you alone.* Pretty nifty, and it has also been shown at Great Smoky Mountains National Park to lead to less mortality than other methods," says Anne Braaten, bear biologist for the National Park Service's North Cascades complex.

Does On-Site Release Work?

Before Great Smoky Mountains National Park began to focus on on-site release, they did 35 relocations from the Chimneys picnic area alone in just three years. In the 14 years between 1991 and 2004 they relocated just 16 bears, most of them during one year when the park suffered a major food failure. That's going from an average of a dozen bears a year to a little more than one bear annually. Over that same time period they handled 43 individual bears, capturing and releasing them on-site 59 times (some bears are more persistent than others).

Rescued as an injured cub, this bear was successfully returned to the park in 2005 after a final hip repair.
© Emily Guss, GSMNP

"Our job is to protect the resources. We believe if we're killing bears and moving bears, we're not doing our job right. We've failed," says Bill Stiver, Supervisory Wildlife Biologist at Great Smoky Mountains National Park.

Success of On-Site Release of Nuisance Black Bears

Research conducted by the University of Tennessee in 1997–98 showed that 73 percent of bears that had on-site workups and releases did not require relocation from the site for at least one year. A follow-up study in 2003 showed that bears captured and released on-site had a much higher survival rate than relocated bears. Female bears had even higher survival rates and were later observed with cubs of their own. On-site release will not be as effective if human-food attractants are still around.

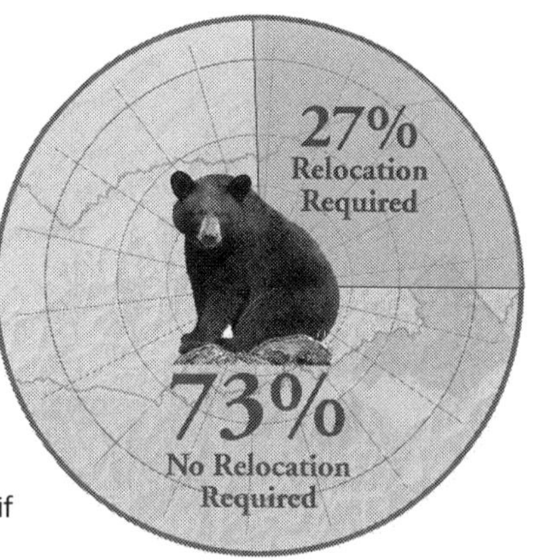

Karelian Bear Dogs

The Wind River Bear Institute in Florence, Montana, is home to the internationally recognized Karelian Bear Dog Partners in Life Bear Shepherding® program founded by biologist Carrie Hunt in 1996. Wind River pioneered an innovative program that uses highly trained dogs and equally trained human handlers to teach bears to recognize and avoid potential conflicts with humans.

Today Wind River's Karelian Bear Dogs (affectionately known as KBDs by their handlers) are in use in Montana, Washington, Nevada, Wyoming, California, Alberta, British Columbia, and even Japan.

Washington's Department of Fish and Wildlife has been partnering with Wind River's KBDs since 2003 when their first dog Mishka arrived and went to work. Today Washington's KBD team includes six dogs partnered with five very dedicated biologists and wildlife officers statewide.

For the agency, the dogs have delivered everything they hoped for and much more. They are commonly used to aversively condition black bears involved in a human-conflict situation. Sometimes hazing is all that's needed to teach the bear a life-saving lesson to leave people places alone. But in situations where attractants are luring in

"On-site" means as close to where the bear was captured as possible. KBDs can be used on or off leash as circumstances dictate. *© Rich Beausoleil*

bears and captured bears are candidates for on-site release, the dogs encourage the bear to quickly head back to the woods. Once the bear has obliged, it's immediately left alone, so it ends up being punished for getting into a conflict situation and rewarded for going back to its natural surroundings. The dogs are highly effective at their jobs.

What the agency didn't expect was all the other ways the KBDs help fulfill the program's mission of "Helping People, Helping Wildlife." They assist with tracking and radio collaring for agency research projects, finding injured and orphaned wildlife, and locating the remains of illegally taken wildlife. The dogs located a black bear involved in a rare attack on a human within 15 minutes of being on the scene, helping restore calm to the local community. And they tracked a bloodied pit bull to a local residence, debunking what the dog's owner later confessed was a fabricated story of a mountain lion attack on a human. They're even used on-leash to haze bighorn sheep and moose away from roads and people.

The people of Washington State are very supportive of non-lethal solutions for resolving human-wildlife conflicts, and have enthusiastically embraced the KBD program. The dogs are constantly used in outreach and education, and are probably the most popular ambas-

Carl Lackey's Karelian Bear Dog encourages a 500-pound bear to head back to the woods.
© John Humphreys

sadors a wildlife agency could have. They generate reams of positive publicity for WDFW.

Even better news for any cash-strapped agency dealing with budget cutbacks, the Washington KBD program is entirely funded by private donations. A KBD program involves a big commitment by the handlers and the full support of the agency. Unlike a lot of tools of the trade, the dogs are on duty 24/7 and can't be put back in the closet when they're not needed. Anyone interested in looking into using KBDs should talk to someone who's already doing so.

Early Intervention: Does It Work?

Nevada's long-time bear biologist Carl Lackey reports a much higher success rate in modifying conflict behavior and saving the bear if they can intervene when the bear is just beginning to explore human-provided food sources. He asks people to call and report any problems immediately so they can trap and tag the bear, then release it at or near the capture location, sending it on its way in a hail of non-lethal projectiles and chased by trained Karelian Bear Dogs. According to Lackey, early intervention has helped save more than 400 bears.

"It's a lot easier to teach a young kid that stealing pencils is bad than to wait until he's graduated into breaking into homes. We're very proactive with our bears, and try to catch them at the stealing-pencils phase," said retired supervisory wildlife biologist, Kim DeLozier, of Great Smoky Mountains National Park.

In a four-year study in Sequoia and Kings Canyon National Park, aversive conditioning reduced but didn't eliminate the occurrence of bears entering developed areas to forage on human food and trash. It was most effective on wild bears; for food-conditioned bears, effectiveness was directly related to how quickly a bear's first experience with human food was followed by a lesson in avoidance. In this study, aversive conditioning was least effective on yearling bears, and most effective on adults that had never, or only rarely, gotten human-food rewards.

One Bear at a Time

Solving problems one bear at a time can be expensive and time intensive. It's not practical or even possible to use aversive conditioning on every bear in every situation. And no amount of aversive conditioning will work long-term if the source of the problem isn't eliminated.

But for bears that have a good chance of learning their lesson and heading back to the wild, aversive conditioning can be a real life saver. There's also evidence that aversive conditioning can break the chain of mother bears teaching their offspring to rely on human food sources. So when mom has a negative experience, she'll pass her new-found distaste for human places along to her cubs, instead of her mental map to all the best spots to find garbage or other human-provided treats.

Do-It-Yourself Aversive Conditioning

Aversive or negative conditioning that involves the use of trained dogs, pyrotechnics, beanbag rounds and other tactics is generally administered by trained professionals or those who have been properly trained by their wildlife management agency. See Chapter 21 for tactics anyone can use to respond to unwelcome black bears. Leave dealing with grizzly bears to the experts. ❖

"You find bears in town because that's where there's a lot of food. We're partnering with Colorado Parks and Wildlife to teach people how to avoid attracting bears," says Bryan Peterson, President of Bear Smart Durango.

8

Laying Down the Law

A well-meaning couple in Oysterville, Washington, was spending upwards of $4,000 a year on dog food. But they weren't feeding dogs; they were feeding nearly a dozen black bears.

At first they thought the bears were "cute." But eventually hungry bears that had gotten way too comfortable around people were breaking down garage doors, wrecking freezers, and taking down fences in their quest for more of the handouts they'd grown accustomed to.

"It's pretty frightening when four or five adult bears show up on your front porch all at the same time," one anxious neighbor told the *Chinook Observer* in June 2010.

At the time it was not illegal in Washington to feed bears or other wildlife, but it was still foolish and highly irresponsible. It could have gotten people killed. It did get bears killed.

All told, a record 10 black bears were removed from the property, including seven adults and three cubs. They were lured into traps with food they knew all too well: pastries, donuts and other treats. Five of the captured bears had been fed by humans since they were cubs, and were far too "tame" to survive in the wild. So even though they were very healthy, the Washington Department of Fish and Wildlife had no choice. The bears were killed and the meat was donated to homeless shelters.

Two other adults and the three cubs were eventually relocated;

encouraged to high tail it off into the woods by two of Washington's highly trained Karelian Bear Dogs.

"Maybe if there'd been an anti-feeding law then, someone would have reported the situation. If we could have intervened sooner we probably could have saved all the bears," explained Rich Beausoleil, Washington's Bear and Cougar specialist. "The people feeding the bears loved bears. Too bad they loved them to death."

The bears died needlessly, but as it turned out, they did not die in vain. WDFW had tried for several years in a row to get an anti-feeding law passed by the state legislature. But year after year there was always some part of the bill that someone took issue with. It was always "wait until next year."

The Oysterville story was widely publicized; the good citizens of Washington State were outraged by the needless destruction of so many bears brought on by people who "were doing nothing illegal." The time was right to push for meaningful change.

A new bill was crafted that was acceptable to most stakeholders because it was highly focused and targeted only large carnivores. The WDFW took their case to the natural resources committee. A powerful presentation peppered with photos from the scene told a tale too gut-wrenching to ignore.

Today intentionally feeding bears in Washington carries a fine of up to $1,000 per instance; even unintentionally feeding bears ("I had no idea bears were attracted to empty beer cans...") can cost you $87.

Once people understand the real problems that cause human-bear conflicts and the equally real consequences of allowing them to go unsolved, many people are willing to do their part. But as always seems the case, a few may need some extra motivation. Sometimes just the threat of getting ticketed and fined is all it takes to move people to action.

"Our research revealed that agencies with a law allowing them to fine people said it worked, and they wanted to be able to levy stiffer fines so it would work even better. Agencies that didn't have that ability were envious. Unfortunately sometimes you have to hit people in the pocketbook to make them wake up and smell the coffee," said Rich Beausoleil.

About half of all North American wildlife management agencies can cite a statute, policy or law that makes it illegal to intentionally or unintentionally feed bears by allowing them access to human food, garbage, pet food, birdseed and other attractants. Some statutes are mostly bark; others have a lot of bite.

The granddaddy of anti-feeding regulations aimed at reducing human-bear conflicts is probably the West Yellowstone, Montana, ordinance enacted in 1987 and since revised and strengthened several times. Today the West Yellowstone police chief has the legal right to mandate trash pickup times that ensure garbage will not be sitting out overnight, require non-bear-resistant containers to be securely stored inside a building and perhaps even more importantly, to educate the public. Many towns and municipalities have borrowed these basic building blocks and created ordinances that work for them.

In some areas where bear populations are now expanding, parks and communities have proactively passed regulations and laws, deciding that prevention would be much easier and, in the long run, much more effective and affordable than dealing with problems.

But all too often it takes cataclysmic events like Oysterville that create a public outcry before people say "enough is enough," and start pushing for change instead of resisting it.

Scenes like this bear that had to be killed in Leavenworth, Washington, helped hammer home the point that Oysterville was not an isolated incident. *© Rich Beausoleil*

In Snowmass, Colorado, it was the accidental death of a cub that was being tranquilized along with its mother and littermate so the human-food conditioned family could be relocated.

On the California side of Lake Tahoe, a tourist whose garbage was attracting a big male bear was issued a permit to have the bear trapped and killed. But instead a small mother bear and her two cubs wandered into the trap and ended up dead, their bodies unceremoniously dumped with the garbage.

In Crystal Lakes, Colorado, a volunteer watched a trapped bear waiting for the ultimate solution, and said "No more." In Canmore, Alberta, Canada, and Whistler, British Columbia, black bears were dying by the hundreds for no good reason. In Yosemite a reporter witnessed a bear's last moments on earth and told a poignant story that went viral well before the term was even invented. The list could go on and on; progress written in the blood of bears and the sweat and sometimes tears of the people responsible for managing them.

"Having a strong anti-feeding regulation gives you a lot of leverage and helps when it comes to bear management, or rather people management," explains Virginia's Black Bear Project Leader Jaime Sajecki. "If you have nine out of ten people in a neighborhood doing the right thing and one who refuses to secure their trash or take down bird feeders, then you can cite them for a violation of the anti-feeding regulation. Usually we don't have to actually write tickets; if saving the bear isn't important to them, the promise of a fine and a ticket gets their attention. If there is one thing I think bear managers need to make their lives easier, it is a good anti-feeding regulation."

Anti-feeding regulations also make life easier for people and communities trying to do the right thing. Sometimes "it's illegal, and if you get caught you'll get slapped with a big fine" just works better than "it's really not a good idea to feed the bears."

Anti-feeding regulations cover more than deliberately feeding bears. These regulations address a wide range of human habits and practices that can result in bears accessing human-provided food sources. They often include mandating bear-resistant garbage containers, dictating how trash is stored and handled, regulating or banning the use of bird feeders, prohibiting residential and municipal landscaping that attracts bears, and requiring bear-resistant storage of livestock feed and treats. A recently added provision in the Pitkin County, Colorado, building codes requires the use of round door knobs bears can't open for all new residential construction. And wildlife agencies across the continent are rooting for a statute that requires folks who raise chickens to keep them locked up at night or safely tucked away behind an electric fence.

There's an excellent sample ordinance plus a worksheet for communities beginning the process of developing an ordinance that works for their particular situation on the *www.bearsmart.com* website under managing communities. You can also download sample ordinances at *www.LivingWithBears.com.* ❖

Bears love these super-sized carryout containers. *© The Humane Society of the United States*

9

Out of Options: When Bears Are Killed

No one wants to see a perfectly healthy bear die, particularly the wildlife managers who have to put the bear down. It's the very worst part of their job; it often literally makes them sick. If you could see the expression on the face of a trapped bear sitting forlornly in a cage awaiting its fate, it would make you sick too. Because most of the time the bear's death could have been avoided. Instead it's paying the ultimate price for human carelessness, ignorance, or indifference.

Unfortunately every bear can't be saved. And the more problems there are, the less tolerant of bears people become. Soon every bear gets painted with the same behavioral brush and people just want them all to be eliminated. Once a bear has crossed the line and is endangering human safety, removing it from the population is usually the only option.

Lethal removal is often referred to an euthanasia. That's because when wildlife managers are forced to destroy a bear, they do so in the most humane way possible, generally by lethal injection or a well-placed bullet to the brain. But people think of euthanasia as mercy killing—something you do when your pet is suffering and you're putting it out of its misery. Most bears that are euthanized are perfectly healthy. So that's why I say killed instead of euthanized, as do a growing number of bear managers. The consequences of living or playing irresponsibly in bear country aren't pretty.

Bear managers have strict guidelines about when and how to remove a bear from the population. Guidelines vary by state and region. In areas where bears are not an accepted part of the landscape, lethal removal can be triggered by something as simple as a bear wandering into someone's backyard. If you live in one of those places, ignorance is the enemy and education is a bear's best friend. The first step is helping people understand what causes problems and what can be done to prevent them.

"When bears must be killed, agencies shouldn't hide it. You need to use it as a learning experience, explain to people what led to it and why you were forced to do it. Many people will be furious, as I am when I'm forced to kill a healthy bear. People need to understand that these bears are victims of their communities or wherever they were continually attracted by and rewarded with food," explains Rich Beausoleil.

Solving the Real Problems

The most challenging part of human-bear management is focusing on the big picture: identifying the root causes of problems and figuring out practical ways to prevent them. That's mostly what the rest of this book is about.

Some aspects of proactive bear management focus on keeping both people and bears out of trouble—such as temporarily closing a problematic campground or trail or an area bears frequent at certain times because food is abundant and bears are hungry. And encouraging bear-smart land development and landscaping and building codes.

Other tactics range from education to inspiration to legislation. Solving the real problems means protecting natural habitat, eliminating things that attract bears, and finding effective ways to keep bears out of and away from any and all human-provided food sources.

Coming up with long-term solutions to the problems that create human-bear conflicts is a process. It requires a lot of research, education and persuasion, as well as acceptance of responsibility and long-term commitment from people and communities. Changing attitudes, habits and actions is never easy. But it's the only way to cure the disease instead of just treat the symptoms.

As is almost always the case, a couple of pounds of prevention are much more effective than a ton of reaction. Public education, participation, and support is a must if conflict prevention is going to work. That's why today most bear managers spend so much of their time working with people.

How You Can Help

Wildlife management agencies juggle complex responsibilities and answer to many masters. The fact that the public thinks moving bears or killing bears solves problems makes it harder for agencies to get the approval and funding they need to use preventative programs and management techniques that may be more effective.

Public pressure can be a powerful force for change. So if you live or play in bear country, step up to the plate. Get smart about bears. Lock up your trash. Take down your bird feeders. Clean up your act. Inspire your neighbors. Galvanize your community. Appeal to your legislatures to implement regulations like bear-resistant trash ordinances, bird-feeding restrictions and other regulations that will reduce conflicts and promote peaceful coexistence. Get involved and be part of the solution instead of part of the problem. ❖

© Bill Lea

I Hold the Smoking Gun

By Chris Parmeter, Wildlife Manager, Gunnison District, Colorado

First appeared in the *Durango Herald*

It was 3:30 a.m. The acrid smell of gunpowder lingered in the air, mixed with the sweet, sickening smell of bear blood that oozed down the driveway of the home. The blood looked black illuminated in the glow of the porch light and the wavering beams of our flashlights. The bear was also black—big, black and now, lifeless.

I wish that it hadn't ended up this way—the bear's final agonized writhing in the driveway, the smoking shotgun, my hands shaking from the rush of adrenaline and emotion. Unfortunately, neither of us had much say in the matter. This tragic end had been decided long ago.

This is part of my job as a district wildlife manager, a part that I despise. Dozens of wildlife officers must perform this same awful duty every year throughout Colorado. Some bears, no doubt, must be killed. But many of these incidents can be avoided if people used some common sense.

I knew this end would come, long before he did. I met him three years ago, when he was just a cub. He was trapped in a dumpster that his mother led him into to eat.

I lifted him out with a snare pole and let him go. He was freed from the confines of the dumpster, but he couldn't escape his fate—the end of his story was already being written.

Our paths crossed several times during the next couple of years. He'd pull down bird feeders and I'd give out "Living with Bears" brochures to the homeowners. A month later, I'd see the bird feeders hung again, right against the picture window.

The homeowners would report the bear's "aggressive behavior," how it stood and looked in their window—how it wasn't frightened of people, even as they stood just on the other side of the pane and took pictures of it.

I knew how the bear must have thought, too. Four hours picking berries one by one, versus four minutes munching down birdseed for the same caloric gain. The goofy-looking humans on the other side of the glass had never bothered him, never told him he was trespassing, never tried to stop him, never tried to help him by permanently taking down the bird feeders.

Plainly, that meant the birdseed was his. This side of the window became his turf, not theirs.

Later, we hashed it out over trash cans and dumpsters. He was a good-sized bear by now, handsome and black as the night. In the dark, he was a mere shadow, or more so, a complete absence of light.

He was big enough to upend a dumpster if he felt like it, but more often he just took advantage of the myriad of trash cans left casually, thoughtlessly, out on the street. The complaints would come, and the garbage can owners would all cite the same solution—get rid of the bear.

No one wanted him killed, of course. After all, he had only gotten into their garbage. They just wanted him gone; taken away; moved somewhere else so that they would not have to make any changes in the way they did business. It was convenient for them to put their trash out the night before pickup. Bear-proof trash cans cost $200 or more.

Then finally one night, inevitably, the old bruin took it too far. Lured by a chain of unwitting and apathetic homeowners, urged on by a string of bountiful successes, he was at last coaxed over the line. It all came down with frustrating irony. Not even the backdrop seemed right: a well-kept, rustically adorned summer home in a forested subdivision. Most ironically though, the homeowners who were his final victims did not feed birds, or leave garbage cans on the street, or feed their pets outside or do anything else to draw him in. They did nothing at all to encourage this bloody outcome, but suffered the ugly consequences of their neighbors' neglect and sloth.

In the end, the bear, driven by biology and emboldened by experience, broke through the kitchen window, only to be run back out by the home's rightful occupants. But the bear was determined now, and lingered, and after a while seconded his attempt to hijack the house.

A second roust, more confrontational than the first—involving thrown objects and much yelling—put the bear out again. But he wasn't going to leave until he got what he wanted.

This is when I met this bear for the last time. Our final encounter, considerably less pleasant for both of us over any previous ones, involved two slugs fired from my 12-gauge shotgun into his chest. As he gasped his last breath and his blood oozed out onto the driveway, I only wished that all those people we had met along the way could have been there to share this moment with us. Maybe then...well...

At Home in Bear Country

© Paul Conrad

10

Living in the Bears' Backyard

Once upon a time there were clear dividing lines between the places people lived and the places that still belonged to wild things. Today the places where bears can live and people can't or don't want to are few and far between. People often talk about bears moving closer to town, but in reality it is human development that is perpetually encroaching on bears.

Areas that were once forests, meadows, farmlands and open range have sprouted bumper crops of homes and communities. Entire towns have been carved into the woods, nestled up against the mountains, and draped around the lakes and streams. In much of the country

virtually every wildland area of any size is surrounded by mile after mile of medium- and low-density homes or small hobby farms and ranches. This wildland urban interface, dubbed the WUI, is where people and bears most often cross paths.

Bears don't have much choice about where they live, but people do. If you choose to live in the bears' backyard, it's up to you to learn how to do so responsibly. Bears have proved again and again that they can adapt to our presence and live peacefully among us, going about the business of being bears without disrupting the daily lives of their human neighbors. Unfortunately people often prove to be far less adaptable than bears.

Some biologists say bears are naturally afraid of us; others prefer to characterize their tendency to avoid us as an instinctive wariness of another large predator. Either way the result is the same: most of the time most bears give people a wide berth.

But if high-quality natural foods are in short supply, or people offer up a bottomless bounty of calories that seem like easy pickings, a bear's drive to survive can overcome its natural tendency to stay away from people. If bears test the boundaries and are rewarded for their efforts, they learn to seek us out rather than avoid us. Bears that learn to associate people with food almost always end up in trouble.

Top Causes of Human-Bear Conflicts at Home

- Ignorance, laziness and the attitude: "What are the chances of that happening?" or "It's not my problem."
- Accessible garbage and trash
- Bird feeders and beehives
- Gardens, fruit trees and natural food sources
- Chickens and small, accessible livestock
- Pet food, horse and livestock feed
- Barbecue grills and outdoor kitchens
- Open doors, windows and garages

- Vehicles with food or trash inside
- Ponds, pools and water sources

Workable Ways to Reduce Bear Conflicts at Home

- Make garbage inaccessible: store inside a sturdy building or a bear-resistant container or enclosure.
- Put trash out the morning of pickup, never the night before. Bring cans back inside before nightfall.
- Don't feed birds between the first day of spring and Halloween; don't feed other wildlife at all.
- Bring small livestock (chickens, goats, sheep) into a sturdy locked building, lidded enclosure, or electric-fenced pen at night.
- Pick tree fruits before they ripen. Pick up fallen fruit daily.
- Avoid planting fruit trees, berry bushes and edible (to a bear) gardens near your home.
- Store pet food and livestock feed in a sturdy locked building. Don't leave bowls of food outside.
- Don't keep freezers or refrigerators on your porch or deck or in the garage unless the building is very sturdy with solid doors. Never leave coolers outside.
- Keep garage doors closed and lock up at night, especially if your garage is connected to your home.
- Close and lock bear-accessible windows at night.
- Don't store birdseed, pet food, canned goods or beverages on your deck or porch. Screens don't deter bears.
- Make sure your vehicles don't smell like food. Don't leave wrappers, cans, sunscreen or anything that could smell intriguing inside. Use a pine or odor-eliminating air freshener. Keep windows rolled up and doors locked.
- Consider electric fencing to protect gardens, beehives, fruit trees, chicken coops, livestock, and even part-time residences.

Are You a Source of Anthropogenic Food?

Lots of bear literature talks about the perils of providing bears with anthropogenic food sources, but seldom defines just what that means. Anthropogenic means "of, relating to, or resulting from the influence of human beings on nature." For practical purposes, anthropogenic food sources can be anything from a dumpster full of garbage to an orchard full of fruit trees. If food doesn't occur naturally and without human assistance, it's anthropogenic.

Lock It or Lose It

If you're one of the millions of people who leave their vehicles parked outside, don't leave anything inside that could attract a bear. Besides foods and beverages, that includes empty bottles, cans and packages, gum, mints, suntan lotion, lip balm, scented products, and emergency energy bars. And lock your doors. Enterprising bears can easily open most car doors and let themselves in. Unfortunately doors generally close and lock behind them, and bears are forced to chew and claw their way out.

Snowmass Village Animal Services, Colorado

Floridian Randy Moon woke up one night, looked out and saw what he thought was an intruder rummaging through his daughter's car. When he went outside he discovered the intruder was a black bear that had opened an unlocked door, climbed in, and then managed to lock itself inside. By the time Randy opened a door and the bear finally escaped, the inside of the car was totaled. As often happens, Moon discovered that his insurance didn't cover wildlife damage. There was no food inside the car, but bears had been attracted to the Moon's property by accessible garbage and a pig the family was raising.

Ursus Urbanus: Bears in the 'Hood

We humans are creating a whole new subspecies of bear I've nicknamed *Ursus urbanus*. These bears sleep by day and roam through parking lots, alleys, and backyards at night, growing fat on a steady supply of calories. They're bigger than wild bears, reproduce at a younger age, and die from unnatural causes well before their time. Despite the fact that litters are larger, far fewer cubs survive long enough to strike out on their own. Some urban bears don't even bother denning up; why turn in when the food supply never dries up?

Researchers Jon Beckmann and Joel Berger tracked radio-collared bears in the Tahoe Basin as part of a comprehensive long-term study in cooperation with the Nevada Department of Wildlife. They spent many a night following their subjects from parking lot to parking lot watching while the bears fished in dumpsters and garbage cans for their dinner. Necropsies (the bear version of an autopsy) showed that their stomachs were filled with garbage, packaging and assorted other human junk.

These areas in and around urban centers are referred to as urban sinks. Bears are lured to urban sinks by what Nevada's bear biologist Carl Lackey calls clumped urban food resources: lots of calorie-filled dumpsters and trash cans. They're the urban version of a salmon run, but the "salmon" never stop running. Bears concentrate around these dependable food sources, grow faster and fatter, but often pay with their lives for living high off the garbage. Death rates in urban sinks are much higher than birth and survival rates. Allowing urban sinks to exist is a recipe for bear disaster. Watch "Urban Bears: Keeping Nevada's Bears Wild" on YouTube for an eye-opening look at living with urban and suburban bears.

Traits of Ursus Urbanus

- Grows larger than wild bears. In one study, a few of the bears tipped the scales at more than 500 pounds, nearly twice the size of the average adult male in the Tahoe Basin.
- Spends less time foraging; 8.5 hours vs. more than 13 hours a day for wild bears. They're not lazy; they just can't eat any more.
- Naps during the day and works the night shift when humans are sleeping and the pickings are easier.
- Spends 42 fewer days denning or does not den at all.
- Gives birth to more cubs per litter at a younger age.
- Concentrated food sources result in very small overlapping home ranges and very high bear densities that increase the potential for human-bear conflicts. Bear densities in urban sinks were three times greater than in the wild, resulting in the second-highest bear density in North America.
- Have a much higher mortality rate than wild bears. In one study 65 percent of female cubs died before they were 15 months old; more than three-quarters of the cubs were killed by motor vehicles. No female bears made it past their tenth birthday. ❖

Ursinomorphizing: Taking Advantage of How Bears View People

by Anne Braaten, Bear Management Biologist, North Cascades National Park

People projecting human attributes to other species is anthropomorphizing. It is logical that since bears can only know their own behavioral expectations and thought processes, they view the world through an "ursinomorphizing" filter: they appear to respond to humans much as they would other bears. Their 'natural' initial response is to give us wide berth, as though we were dominant bears.

What they learn from us is how much leeway we'll give them. One thing people miss is how big a deal it is for a bear to show itself to someone it would presumably think was a dominant individual, albeit a different species. Subordinate bears give wide berth to dominant bears. If they test us by leaving cover and coming closer to people, and people allow them to do so, they have just learned that they can be in close proximity with people. From there they may ramp up their testing of people until they learn they are safe near us, and some bears may extend this to pushing us around as if they were the dominant bear. This can happen in the course of hours. And this is how they end up dead.

I ask people to try to look at the world through a bear's eyes. Bears live in an intrinsically social system where they move around each other as the social ladder dictates. They are also out there making a living on the best of whatever they can find. If they find your food, your pet's food, your horse's feed, the bird feeder, the garbage can—they are doing what bears do: finding the calories they need to live not just through the summer, but also through winter. It is natural for them to seek out easy sources of food, because they do not eat while hibernating for several months. Think of it as "eat more, exercise less": they will naturally prefer your 1,600-calorie suet block to something they need to work harder for.

Of course we need to make these things unavailable to bears, but people also need to realize that it's O.K. to assert dominant behavior by yelling, clapping their hands or otherwise making noise from the safety of a porch or window. Discouraging a bear from hanging around isn't "harassing" it; it's merely asserting your personal space, something bears understand. Following these simple principles can help keep bears out of your way, and could save their lives.

11

Tackling Trash: The Number One Problem

Why Bears Love Garbage

Many people have a hard time understanding why bears are attracted to icky, stinky trash. It's because just one typical 35-gallon garbage container filled with leftovers and scraps can provide more than enough calories in an hour or two to feed a bear for a day or even a week.

Bears are just like people. It's calories eaten (food) minus calories expended (exercise and basic metabolism) that determines how much a bear weighs. But while people often struggle to lose weight, bears spend most of their time trying to eat as much as possible. That's because bears need to gain 30 to 40 percent of their springtime body

© Kathie Waibel

weight by late fall if they're going to survive winter hibernation. Talk about a ticking time bomb. If you woke up in April and had to gain 100 pounds by the end of October or die, you'd do whatever it took to fatten up.

So will bears. Imagine the bear bounty offered by a trip down an alley filled with overflowing trash cans or a ramble through backyards dotted with bird feeders. If we make it easy for bears to fatten up on the leftovers of the human good life, how can we blame them for taking advantage of an easy meal?

Now think like a bear. You gave birth to two cubs and nursed them through the winter while going hungry yourself for five or six months. You worked hard all summer trying to find enough food to keep your rambunctious offspring growing like weeds and to fatten yourself up for the winter. The drought ruined most of the berry crop. If you don't find enough food soon, you put yourself and your cubs at risk of starvation. Or you're a teenager on your own for the first time. You're hungry, lonely and searching everywhere for anything with calories. Now it's a race against the clock. You're blessed with a nose that can lead you to food many miles away. Your only choice is to follow it.

"Garbage Kills Bears" is a slogan used all over North America to make people understand that letting a bear get into the trash just once is often the beginning of the end for that bear.

A cub learns a lethal lesson.
© Mike Fox

Why Garbage Kills Bears

Getting rewarded for getting into garbage is often a pivotal event in a bear's life. Lured in by the smell of food, the bear overcomes its natural wariness of humans. If it gets the reward it came looking for and goes away none the worse for the experience, it will come back to the all-you-can-paw-through buffet.

Bears are "opportunistic feeders." That means they'll try anything once, and if it's edible, they'll check out the surrounding area to see if there's more. Anything that smells promising is fair game.

Pretty soon the clever and enterprising bear is causing a lot of "problems" for people. As it gets more comfortable around people, it grows bolder. It might start strolling through backyards in the middle of the day, pushing open screen doors, or popping out open or unlocked windows searching for more food. In some areas bears have even learned to open car doors in search of treats. Soon the bear gets labeled a "nuisance." Eventually it may cause so much damage, or become so assertive and possessive of the human food sources it has come to rely on, a wildlife manager will be forced to kill it. All because someone who lives in bear country wouldn't lock up their trash.

It's Not the Bears That Are Nuisances and Problems

The term "nuisance" or "problem" bear originated many decades ago when situations were evaluated strictly from the human point of view. If wildlife activity was annoying or bothersome or just getting in the way of "progress," the wildlife was deemed a nuisance and subject to removal. Today wildlife management is much more enlightened, but wildlife vocabulary remains mired in the dark ages. The media loves short catchy phrases, so "nuisance bear" and "problem bear" have become common descriptors. The problem with the terminology is that it puts the blame squarely on the bear. But in the vast majority of cases, problems with bears are caused by people intentionally or unintentionally attracting them.

"Nuisance bear is a term that needs to be wiped out of our wildlife management vocabulary. The educational value alone that would result from people realizing that conflicts with wildlife are almost entirely the result of human actions would justify any amount of work necessary to change our way of thinking and talking and managing," says Rich Beausoleil.

Bear-Resistant Solutions

Bears can easily open standard metal and rubber trash containers, even ones with locking lids. Defeating bungee cords or a brick-weighted lid is a snap for an animal that can easily rip apart a tree.

Using a bear-resistant container (BRC) is an almost sure-fire way to defeat determined bears. BRCs come in a wide range of sizes, from 64 gallons to dumpster size, and range in price from around $100 to $500 or more. It may seem like a lot of money for a trash container, but it's a small investment compared to the price of replacing containers and cleaning up after a bear, week after week. It's an even smaller investment compared to a bear's life.

Going bear-resistant can meet resistance from trash haulers, because many BRCs have to be opened manually, which slows down pickups. And homeowner associations trying to protect neighborhood aesthetics may have to be persuaded to amend their lists of approved containers.

Times change, rules and procedures can too. Sometimes people just need to understand why the old ways don't work anymore, and get introduced to new ones that do. Some trash haulers will partner with communities to come up with practical ways to go bear-resistant. Some enlightened communities provide bear-resistant containers for a small monthly fee.

"We have been using the Kodiak carts since 2012 on the Flathead

After many years of testing and experimenting, a fully-automated bear-resistant polycart (IGBC certified) is now available from Kodiak Products. *www.kodiak-products.com*

Indian Reservation in Montana, with no entry from black or grizzly bears or other scavengers," says George Barce, wildlife biologist for CSKT (Confederated Salish and Kootenai Tribes). "The local disposal company (Republic Services/Allied Waste) likes the performance of the carts so much that they've purchased several hundred to use here as well as in their other service areas. The drivers go through a relatively short learning phase to find out just what they have to do to open the can. The key to getting the Kodiak carts out on the ground is having disposal companies willing to take the time to learn how they operate. Allied has been a good partner in this endeavor."

The most dependable bear-resistant containers are those that have earned a thumbs-up from the Interagency Grizzly Bear Committee's Product Testing Program that was started back in 1989. Commercial products ranging from standard-sized trash cans to dumpsters are submitted to the center for rigorous visual inspections before facing the real thing.

The Grizzly and Wolf Discovery Center in West Yellowstone, Montana, is home to a number of grizzly bears that put bear-resistant products to the ultimate test. Some of the Center's bears were

Manufacturers send trash containers to the Center for the ultimate grizzly test.
© Grizzly & Wolf Discovery Center

orphaned as cubs, and wouldn't have survived on their own in the wild. Other bears had learned that people equal food and were paroled to the Center instead of being destroyed. The bears have individual dens, and roam around a two-acre outdoor habitat where visitors can watch them. Their keepers hide food under rocks and in log piles to encourage them to use their natural foraging skills.

The bears earn a living trying their best to get at the food treats hidden inside the trash containers and dumpsters sent to the Center for testing. Grizzly bears are incredibly strong, as well as curious and patient. A grizzly can punch a hole in a cabin roof, rip the door off a car, or pry open just about anything it can get its claws under. A garbage container that can resist the efforts of a persistent grizzly is one tough container.

Visit IGBC at *www.igbconline.org* for the most current listing of approved bear-resistant products.

More Than One Way to Outsmart a Bear

Bear issues in Leavenworth, Washington, dropped dramatically when the town's garbage service changed its schedule. They used to pick up trash very early in the morning, causing even the most committed people to put it out the night before. In 2012 the town switched to picking up trash mid-afternoon, and problems with bears and garbage went way down.

Central collection sites with bear-resistant dumpsters can keep garbage—and bears—off of neighborhood streets. *© Bryan Peterson, Bear Smart Durango*

HOW TO KEEP BEARS OUT OF YOUR TRASH

Put Your Trash Out in the Morning

Sure, it's easier to take your trash out to the curb the night before. But letting garbage sit out overnight is inviting hungry bears to come and get it. If natural foods are in short supply or there are juvenile bears in the area just learning to forage on their own that invitation can be hard to turn down.

The town of Payson, Arizona, studied the issue many years ago, and found that residents who left their garbage out overnight had a 70 percent chance of attracting a bear. That chance dropped to just two percent for people who put their trash out the morning of pickup. If you don't put it out, they can't come and get it. And whatever else is lying around.

Carelessness and complacency can be fatal. Don't be responsible for starting a bear down a path that leads to conflicts, problems, and all too often the death of a bear whose only crime was being hard-working and hungry. Use a BRC or get up five minutes earlier and put your trash out in the morning.

Give Your Trash Cans a Bath

A good spray-down with bleach or ammonia will help eliminate lingering odors that can attract bears, so spray your cans inside and out after every pickup during bear season. Some people attach a mesh bag of moth balls, a rag soaked in ammonia, or an industrial-strength odor-eliminating air freshener to the inside of the lid. Avoid pleasant scents like lemon and vanilla that can attract bears instead of deter them.

Stash Your Trash Securely

It won't do much good to take your trash out in the morning if you store it in an old garbage can next to your garage the rest of the week. Under decks, on screened-in porches, in a flimsy shed or garage, or in

© Bryan Peterson, Bear Smart Durango

the back of your pickup truck are also bad places to store garbage.

In between collection days or trips to the dump, store garbage inside the house or in a sturdy garage, shed or barn with solid doors that close and lock with no gaps big enough to get a claw under. If the building has lever-style door handles, be sure to lock it up each night, or replace the handles with old-fashioned round knobs that bears can't open. Avoid storing trash under windows and next to exterior doors.

You can leave a BRC outside as long as it's latched at all times; secured to a sturdy post is even better. Because it still looks (and smells) like trash, it will still attract bears. After they get tired of trying to defeat it, they may look around for easier pickings. So make sure they don't find any.

Freeze It

If you don't have a secure way to store garbage in between pickups, start a trash sack in the freezer for extra smelly items like fish, meat, chicken, bones and fruit. Add your garbage-popsicle to the trash the morning of pickup, or when you're taking trash to the dump.

Corral Your Trash

A bear-resistant enclosure with a top or roof can hold several trash containers. A sturdy chain link enclosure with a lid that can stand up to being jumped on by a bear, metal flanges and hinges, and a good lock—not a simple latch—will defeat most bears. Bears are great diggers, so build your trash corral on a concrete pad. Go for materials a bear can't claw or bite through—chicken wire or flimsy fencing won't work. Odors from garbage will still attract bears. A daily spray bath with ammonia or a cleaner like Pine Sol can help. In areas with high bear activity, storing trash inside a securely locked building or outbuilding is a better option.

Build Your Own Bear-Proof Trash Center

Longtime District Wildlife Manager Kevin Wright from Snowmass, Colorado, is known for putting the onus for preventing problems squarely on the species that causes most of them (people) and coming up with innovative solutions that work. He says that a specially constructed outbuilding made from concrete or cinder block with heavy-duty wood or steel doors and a roof is a good solution in areas with high bear activity. Sides need to be flush with the ground and there should be no more than a two-inch gap at the bottom of the doors; any wider and a bear can slip a paw under and yank. The weakest point is always the door(s) and the latch; a steel door with a round knob is the most effective. Ventilation holes should be kept to the bare minimum and covered with heavy gauge steel mesh.

"Buildings and enclosures are very effective as long as they are properly secured. We have very few problems with bears breaking into well-built enclosures," says Kevin Wright.

"For a bear, garbage is probably the ultimate food resource. It's available year-round, it's in the same place week after week, and it's replenished after use." — *Jon Beckmann, Wildlife Conservation Society*

DIY Bear-Resistant Trash Containers

Louisiana, Florida and Virginia are among the states now offering detailed guidelines for retrofitting standard trash containers with bear-resistant latches. You can create your own BRC for less than $50 with materials from the hardware store, but your waste disposal company must approve use. The containers passed live black bear testing at the Virginia Tech Black Bear Research Center. Containers haven't been tested with grizzlies. To learn more, please visit *www.dgif.virginia.gov/wildlife/bear/*

Neighborhood Bear Watch

Peer pressure can be a powerful weapon. Once people know their neighbors frown on them creating a situation that could be expensive, unsanitary, unsightly, and potentially dangerous to both bears and people, most folks think twice before they haul 70 gallons of leftovers out to the curb the night before, use their open truck bed for a dumpster, or pile their trash outside their home or garage.

If you can help your neighborhood become a bear-smart place to live, you could save your community a lot of aggravation and expense, improve your property values, and add to the appeal of living in your neighborhood. And you could save a bear's life. ❖

Taking Back the City Streets

Ursus urbanus is not confined to Nevada. Cities all across North America are reporting bear populations that are living quite comfortably in alleys and roaming city streets, growing fat on the leftovers of the good life.

Boulder is nestled into the foothills of Colorado's rapidly growing Front Range. It's a community that's socially liberal, economically well off, and considers itself to be enlightened. People are fiercely protective of their abundant local wildlife, including their bears. Nevertheless western Boulder had long been a hot spot for human-bear conflicts.

The city had been debating what to do about the situation for more than a decade. By 2012 they estimated that there were at least 16 bears living within the city limits. Determined to make the most of the city's passion for protecting their bears, two enterprising Colorado Parks and Wildlife district wildlife managers partnered with the city on an exhaustive two-year study designed to find workable ways for people and bears to coexist.

© Sara Tuttle

A small army of Bear Aware volunteers, CPW staff, and city staff went to work meeting with residents and testing and evaluating programs. They discovered that a combination of education and enforcement produced the most effective tools to motivate change.

In 2013, in the midst of the pilot project, Boulder had a particularly challenging season with bears in town and a record four bears identified as public safety risks were killed. The public's very vocal outrage pushed the City Council into acting even before the pilot project was completed.

In March of 2014 they adopted an ordinance that requires approximately 12,436 residences in western Boulder to secure trash and compost from bears at all times until collected by a trash hauler by using bear-resistant trash cans and storing trash/compost in a secure structure (e.g. garage) or in a bear-resistant enclosure. Fines were increased to $250 for a first-time offense and the city plans to hire additional code enforcement personnel.

Western Disposal worked non-stop to find a cost-effective solution for their customers, and finally managed to come up with a design that defeated the enterprising bears at the Discovery Center in Montana and earned certification from the Interagency Grizzly Bear Committee.

Hats off to District Wildlife Managers Kris Middledorf and Kristin Cannon, CPW and Boulder City staff, the people of Boulder, and all the Bear Aware volunteers who took to the streets to help make it all happen.

Is It Working?

In the first two months of enforcement, Boulder issued 245 notices of violation of its bear-resistant trash container ordinance. Homeowners get a warning, a bear education flier, and a chance to fix the problem. Most quickly comply. The price of not doing so is a $250 fine. Most people in the enforcement zone had bear-resistant containers, but as is universally true, they are only effective when closed and latched.

"Part of what we're trying to do is reduce trash as an attractant, and that seems to be effective," urban wildlife conservation coordinator Val Matheson told the *Boulder Daily Camera.*

Matheson said there isn't enough data to draw strong conclusions, but one interesting trend has already emerged: reports of bear sightings just outside the area where homes are required to have bear-resistant containers have gone up from one to two percent of sightings to more than 10 percent.

The ordinance gives the city manager the authority to extend the zone where bear-resistant containers are required. Matheson said it's not clear yet if people in north Boulder are just more likely to report bear activity now that awareness is higher or if the bears have changed their foraging habits. They will study the statistics and decide whether or not to extend the regulation zone.

Western Disposal CEO Frank Bruno said the company has retrofits approved now for both kinds of containers in use, including a latch on the containers for curbside pickup that's compatible with the automated trucks on those routes.

There have been some complaints about the new containers; most people don't like mandated change. But Western Disposal says there have been far fewer complaints than expected.

They are not sure yet how much the switch will cost customers, but expect it to be far less than the $10 a month they used to charge for a bear-resistant container. Using a retrofit manufactured at the state prison in Cañon City helped Western Disposal keep costs low.

"We feel really proud that we've been able to do this and address a significant public policy goal," Bruno said. "The public and private sector have been able to work together to address issues with wildlife that were of great concern to the community." ❖

12

Home Bear-Smart Home

People who live in cities often install burglar bars on windows, motion detector lights in their yards, and high-tech security systems. Most wouldn't dream of going to sleep with windows and doors unlocked because they know crime is often a matter of opportunity and convenience. They're willing to do what it takes to protect their home and family.

But most folks don't give much thought to what it takes to live smart in bear country. Every year bear break-ins cost homeowners untold hours and many thousands of dollars in damage. Bears that

© Sara Tuttle

break into homes usually pay with their lives. A little preventative care and maintenance can protect your home, your property, and the bears.

Build Secure Storage Sheds, Outbuildings and Barns

© Bryan Peterson, Bear Smart Durango

Anything that smells can attract a bear, from empty cans and bottles to livestock feed and bone meal fertilizer. Flimsy, open or unlocked doors and windows and poor construction make it easy for bears to follow their noses inside. You can upgrade your building or surround it with a good electric fence. Or store things that might attract bears somewhere more secure.

One couple stashed horse cookies in plastic tubs near their round pen for years without incident—until the night the new bear in the neighborhood discovered them and made off with 50 pounds of expensive, high-calorie treats. They found the tooth-marked container in the woods. The only sign of the bear was ample piles of bear scat nearby. But you can bet that bear started checking out every plastic container it came across.

Is Your Garage an Easy Target?

You may not be able to smell frozen food, but bears can, as one couple discovered after filling their garage freezer with elk meat and trout. One night a bear pushed in a panel on the garage door, raided their stash, and had quite a feast. Not only did they lose their meat, they had to replace their garage door.

All the guidelines about windows and doors apply equally to garages. Don't leave your garage door open, even if you'll just be gone for a few minutes. This is doubly important if your garage is attached to your home. If you need an added incentive, law enforcement officers note that many human burglars don't break in; they enter homes through unlocked doors and windows. And keep the door between your home and garage closed and locked.

If you live in an area where there are chronic bear break-ins, consider replacing your garage door with a non-panel model or installing metal shutters that you can slide in place when you're gone overnight. Replacing your garage door will be less expensive than replacing a couple of freezers full of food—and the freezers. And then replacing the garage door.

Panel-style garage doors can be a pushover for a bear after treats on the other side.
© Jaime Sajecki, Virginia Department of Game & Inland Fisheries

Another alternative is to move your extra freezer and frig inside your home and away from doors and windows. Refrigerators and freezers have vents that carry odors to the outside. And in some areas bears have learned that those big white boxes are stuffed full of goodies.

Porches and Decks Can Be Dangerous

Many people store canned goods, beverages, birdseed, and all manner of things that can attract bears on their porches and decks, and then festoon the decks with bird feeders. More than one person has admitted to sitting inside taking photos while a bear ambles across the deck searching for treats. Letting bears get that close to your home is a recipe for mutual disaster. See Chapter 21 for tips on how to safely discourage any bears that come exploring, and keep anything that could be an attractant inside your home or in a secure outbuilding.

Cellar and Trap Doors Are Open Invitations

Think Wizard of Oz. In some parts of rural North America, many homes still have root cellars or storage areas with simple exterior trap doors. These doors are equally simple for bears to open, and what better place to den up for the winter than in a nice, snug, weather-tight cellar? If the owners are away, the bear has plenty of time to make itself at home before settling down for a long winter's nap. One industrious bear in Lake Tahoe dragged pillows and comforters from the master bedroom down to the cellar and made a nice little nest. The bear also emptied the pantry and freezer, and turned the rugs and floors into a litter box. That's good motivation to lock and secure your cellar door.

© Sara Tuttle

Pet Doors Can Let In More Than Dogs and Cats

Many adult black bears can easily fit through a dog door. Tom Beck reported that the standard winter den entrance in Colorado was between 9 and 14 inches high. Even small pet doors can provide access for cubs, allowing mama bear to send the youngsters inside to gather up provisions for a family picnic.

Other wildlife species known to use pet doors include raccoons, opossums, skunks and even coyotes, all of which can do considerable damage or injure people once they're trapped inside.

What's a practical solution? You can have your pet door provide access to a fully lidded and sturdily fenced enclosure and give your pets a predator-proof bathroom break. Or you can lock the door at night, or install a one way door, so pets can get out, but can't get back in. There are also doors that can only be activated by a special electronic pet collar. Just remember the door frame must fit snugly; if bears can get their claws in between the door and the frame, they can easily rip it off altogether.

Trees Make Great Ladders

Both grizzly and black bear cubs can climb trees in the blink of an eye. And even adult black bears are at home in the tree tops. So trim back all tree limbs within 15 feet of upper story decks and windows. In one community bears learned to climb trees that hung over roofs, jump onto the roof and dangle over the edge trying to open a window—all to avoid bear unwelcome mats (see Chapter 15) on the ground level.

Bear Stairs

Bears scamper up staircases with ease. One homeowner in the Crystal Lakes subdivision north of Fort Collins, Colorado, built an ingenious "drawbridge" staircase for his weekend home. (They were highly motivated since they'd had a messy and expensive bear break-in.) Now when they head back to the city after a weekend in the mountains, they raise the drawbridge.

© Tim Halvorson

Close and Lock Your Windows

Close and lock all accessible windows whenever you leave home, and every night before you go to bed. If you leave a window open even a crack, a bear can easily slip a paw underneath and push it open. An unlocked window lets a bear get a claw between the edge of the frame and the windowsill. Screens are for keeping out bugs, not bears; they have the impediment level of a spider web. Single pane windows crack very easily. Replace them with double pane glass and you'll save on your energy bills too.

You can leave upstairs windows open unless there's easy bear access, such as a stairway leading to a second floor deck or a handy climbable tree that overhangs the roof. Heat rises, so the heat from downstairs will flow up and out, and cool evening air will eventually flow in.

If you want to keep your downstairs windows open at night, or your home is only occupied intermittently, you can install sturdy grates or bars on the outside of any accessible windows. There are lots of decorative choices today. As an added bonus, they will help keep out human intruders as well. Strategically placed unwelcome mats are another effective option, especially if you don't have to worry about children or pets stepping on one (see Chapter 15).

© Bill Lea

If you share space with savvy bears and your ground floor windows offer a view into the kitchen or pantry, consider closing the blinds or curtains so a bear can't peek in. Windows at ground level should be secured; sturdy grates are your best protection.

A bear tornado going through your home can be almost as destructive as a real one. And animal damage is not always covered by homeowners insurance. *Left: A kitchen from Snowmass Village, Colorado. Right: A former oak antique ice chest. © Doug Bjorlo*

Lose the Lever Door Handles

People like doors with lever handles because they're stylish and easy to open. Bears only care about the easy-to-open part. Nimble and clever, bears quickly learn to push down on the handle and quietly let themselves into the house. Lock your doors or replace your lever handles with sturdy round knobs bears can't get a grip on.

© Sara Tuttle

It also helps if doors open out, rather than in; that way the bear has to pull the door open rather than just lean into it and collapse into your house.

Weird Things That Attract Bears

Bears are insatiably curious and will explore anything they don't recognize in case it might be good to eat. There are also many things with zero nutritional value which give off odors that mimic or resemble food and attract bears.

Formaldehyde Smells Like Ants. Ants are a favorite food for bears; all those little protein-packed insects are full of calories. Ant colonies give off formic acid. So does anything insulated with a material made with formaldehyde. That often includes hot tub covers, bicycle and snowmobile seats, refrigerators and freezers, and insulated vinyl materials of all types. So a bear poking around your hot tub may think it's found the world's biggest ant hill. You can replace your cover with one made of aluminum or something else that does not contain formaldehyde.

© Bear Smart Durango

Petroleum Products Are Strangely Attractive. "For some reason, wide arrays of petroleum-based smells, including lantern and propane stove fuel, attract bears. In fact, the additive put in natural gas to give it a noticeable odor has been used to successfully lure in bears during bait-trapping operations," explains bear biologist Tom Beck.

Citronella products contain a compound that is very attractive to bears. Citronella candles and bug sprays are best avoided. In fact many scented products from air fresheners and candles to scented sun tan lotions can attract bears. We once responded to a bear call and concluded that the bear had ripped off the plywood siding in order to get into a room that was filled with vanilla and fruit-scented candles.

NEW CONSTRUCTION TIPS

The opportunity to live closer to nature and wildlife is one of the biggest reasons people move out into bear country. That opportunity comes with the responsibility to live your dreams without endangering the wildlife that has to share space with you.

Building or remodeling a home in bear country gives you a great opportunity to build-in bear-proofing features that will help prevent problems and improve life for you and the bears in your neighborhood.

To find out about the level of bear activity in your area, talk to your state or provincial wildlife agency as well as your neighbors. Don't rely on your builder or real estate agent; most are not anxious to tell clients about bears and other wildlife, wildfires, water shortages, insect infestations or other facts of life on the wilder side that could seem like warts on the perfect face of Paradise.

If you have a choice of building sites, pick one well away from brush, vegetation, streams, berry patches or fruit- or nut-bearing trees. Black bears don't really like being out in the open. The less natural cover that's close by, the less likely it is a bear will come close enough to investigate. Make sure there are no climbable tree limbs within 15 feet of your house that could provide access to upper story windows or decks.

In the western U.S. many people live in areas with limited shade, lots of meadows and shrub lands at lower elevations, and small pockets of conifers on north-facing slopes. It's highly likely that every bear in the area will visit these cool, shady slopes on hot days. Positioning your house well away from any conifer stands will help prevent the bears from visiting you at the same time.

Bear-Smart Landscaping

Fruits and nuts are natural calorie- and nutrient-dense foods that bears will travel great distances to find. Planting fruit- or nut-bearing trees or bushes creates a concentrated food source for bears, so expect frequent visits. Avoid planting shrubs that produce berries of any kind close to your house; bears eat many types of berries that people don't. If you really want fruit trees, locate your orchard well away from your home and protect your trees with an electric fence. Bears really love clover, so avoid planting clover lawns. I know it can be hard to understand why a bear eating a natural food is a problem, but bears don't separate foods into good and bad. Once you attract bears to your property, they'll explore to see what else is around.

Build in Bear-Proofing

Before you build, think about how trash will be handled and stored and where you'll put your pet food, birdseed and anything else that could attract bears. Think about your pets, livestock, gardens and outbuildings. Plan ahead and you won't have to spend money retrofitting after your first bear break-in. Check out Chapter 11 for a bear-proof building design and more ideas. ❖

© Colorado Parks & Wildlife

Part-Time People, Full-Time Bears

If you live in bear country part time, it can be tough to remember to "think like a bear" every time you head back home. But bears don't have second homes. Taking time to be bear smart and posting information for guests and renters can prevent problems and protect your home and property.

Outside Your Vacation Cabin / Home

- Odors of all types attract bears. Take all food, garbage, trash, empty bottles and cans, packaging and recyclables with you. Don't leave insect repellents, citronella candles or other scented products outside.
- Wash out garbage cans and recycling bins and store inside.
- Thoroughly clean and disinfect your BBQ grill, picnic and deck tables.
- Bring in all bird feeders and birdseed, and store in a bear-proof location. Clean up fallen seed or hulls.
- If your area has a history of bear break-ins, install unwelcome mats.

Inside Your Home

- Creating a bear-proof storage area inside your home or garage can be a good solution when it's not practical to take all bear-attractants with you. Use a bear-proof garbage can, or install a sturdy, locked enclosure or locker well away from windows, doors, and exhaust.
- Clean pet dishes and put away.
- Lock all windows and doors in your home and garage, including screen doors and sliding doors. Close curtains, shades and shutters. Drop a metal or wood rod in the track of sliding doors to prevent bears (and humans) from breaking the latch and opening the door.
- Leave unscented odor-removing air fresheners in all rooms.
- Leave a note with your contact information, in case there is a problem.
- **When you leave for the season**, empty the refrigerator and freezer, thoroughly clean and disinfect, and leave an open box of baking soda inside. Store foods, beverages and spices in your locker.
- Store scented products, including toiletries, lotions, sunscreen, lip balm, hair spray, shampoos and soaps, toothpaste, insect repellent, scented candles, and air fresheners in your locker or a sturdy lidded tub.

Two Decades of Bear Smart Success

The Get Bear Smart Society (GBS), headquartered in the resort municipality of Whistler, British Columbia, has been around since 1994 and under the leadership of the indomitable Sylvia Dolson since 1997. Their mission is to create a basic shift in the way people think about bears that allows people and bears to coexist in harmony.

Writing a mission statement is hard; figuring out what it will take to fulfill that mission is even harder. Turning that must-do list into reality is a whole different bear game. Changing people's attitudes, habits, practices, expectations, rules, regulations, and lifestyles isn't something that happens overnight. But GBS' track record of success proves that it can and does happen.

© Sylvia Dolson

One of the keys to that success is getting all the stakeholders involved in the planning, management, and implementation of bear-smart programs and policies, as well as taking ownership of the vital role they must play to make it all work in the real world. To that end GBS forged strong working relationships with the Resort

Municipality of Whistler, the B.C. Conservation Officer Service, the Royal Canadian Mounted Police, and Carney's Waste Systems. Together this broad-based coalition hammered out practical ways to overcome the formidable obstacles facing all tourist and resort communities in bear country, and eventually turned Whistler into one of British Columbia's few certified Bear Smart communities.

GBS works hard to educate, motivate and inspire change. They have specific programs and materials aimed at the general public, non-governmental organizations, government agencies (parks, environment, wildlife), and law enforcement officials (RCMP, municipal bylaw officers, conservation officers) that cover the why, what and how of getting bear smart. And they do it all with just one full-time staff member, several contractors and a small band of hard-working volunteers, advisors, partners and supporters.

GBS offers educational materials for children, hands-on guidelines for residents and recreationists, and more detailed guides and training resources for businesses, policymakers and bear managers. They've also taken a clever approach to fundraising by creating a popular line of educational merchandise which includes games, books and items designed to appeal to tourists, such as photo magnets, postcards and photo note cards. They sell over 20,000 decks of Bear Smart playing cards every year, proving that learning how to be bear smart can be fun. You can order cards and more from their website.

The GBS website is one of the broadest and deepest sources of information about coexisting with bears on the internet. It's no wonder it averages thousands of visitors each month.

Dolson is a pragmatist. She realizes that knowing how to be bear smart and actually behaving in bear smart ways are two different things. So now they're also using community based social marketing tools and employing social media to encourage and reward sustainable changes in behavior. ❖

13

The Birds and the Bears

Feeding birds is one of the most popular hobbies in North America. Feeders provide good winter forage for birds, and countless hours of entertainment for the millions of people who love watching them.

But every year feeding birds kills bears. A study in 2007 showed that more than 80 percent of human-bear conflicts in New York could be traced back to the bear's initial encounter with a bird feeder. Bird feeders are easy for bears to recognize and reach and always filled

A birdfeeder full of black oil sunflower seed provides a bear with thousands of calories for a few minutes' work. *© Nancyjane Bailey*

with highly nutritious food. It's no surprise that bird feeders are often the first rung on that behavioral ladder of progression.

A bear foraging on bird feeders quickly learns that people's yards are a safe and easy source of food. If it's a clever bear, it goes from house to house looking for more goodies. Sooner or later the bear will discover the house where the garbage isn't stored properly, or food or other attractants are easy to get at.

Why Bears Love Bird Feeders

Bird feeders are fast-food for bears. A pound of black-oil sunflower seeds in the shell has 1,740 calories; a feeder that holds 7 pounds of seeds offers a hungry bear more than 12,000 calories. Imagine how hard a bear would have to work to get that many pounds of seeds in the wild.

Hummingbird feeders are just hanging energy drinks. A 32-ounce feeder holds 774 easily digested calories. The less energy a bear spends finding food, the more calories can go into building up those fat reserves. Every bear's goal is to eat the greatest number of calories with the least amount of effort. "Hitting a bird feeder is just time management for a bear. It's no different than you or I hitting the drive-through when we're hungry and in a hurry. Five minutes and you're fed and outta there," explains Rich Beausoleil.

Attract Birds, Not Bears

If you don't hang them up, they can't rip them down.

The most fool-proof way to keep bears out of your bird feeders is to take them down from the first day of spring through Halloween, or whenever bears are normally out of hibernation in your area.

As the Humane Society points out, most birds don't need your help in the summer when they are nesting and rearing their young. You might even be doing more harm than good, because it's important for nestlings to learn to forage and fend for themselves in order to survive. And feeders typically attract a variety of critters that eat birds, including domestic cats, foxes, coyotes, snakes, and birds of prey. Birds are most in need of food in extreme weather conditions and when natural foods are in short supply.

There are many things other than food that will attract birds to your yard. Birds enjoy everything from a bird bath to a pond; if you can create the sound of splashing water, even better. It doesn't have to be elaborate; something as simple as a galvanized wash tub with a rock popping out of the water will attract a wide variety of birds. Check out your local home improvement store for a selection of self-contained and solar-powered water features and water gardens, or visit *www.gardeners.com*.

Even small water features attract a wide variety of birds.

Birds also enjoy a good sand-bath. It's easy to build a sand or dust box for birds and it's fun to watch them toss dust over their wings and wriggle around cleaning their feathers and ridding themselves of parasites. A gravel bed provides birds with a nice supply of "rock teeth" to store in their crops and help them grind up food. And gravel is a lot cheaper than birdseed.

Natural Hummingbird Feeders

Dozens of annuals, perennials, ground covers, vines and trees with flowers attract hummingbirds, butterflies and beneficial bees. Nectar-rich flowers in deep reds and oranges are sure to attract hummingbirds. I've had great luck with calibrachoa, also known as million bells, a kind of small trailing petunia-like flower that dead-heads

itself, blooms all season and is even wind-resistant. In mild climates it's a perennial, but in colder climes it makes a dependable annual. Other good choices: hummingbird vine, trumpet vine, butterfly bush, columbine, delphinium, hollyhock and rose of Sharon. Check with a local nursery to find out which ones will grow best in your area.

Put Up Bird Nesting Boxes

Nesting boxes can provide an opportunity to watch birds most of the spring and summer and can help birds in areas where old trees with nesting cavities are in short supply. Add to the appeal with bird-attractive landscaping and offer some sort of water, and you'll have a three-season bird garden. Put your feeders back outside when the bears turn in for the winter, and enjoy watching the birds all year long. ❖

Know Your Local and State Laws

In some places you can be ticketed and fined for using bird feeders or feeding birds or other wildlife during the time of year when bears are active.

© Bill Levy

Kicking the Curbside Habit

Flanked by spectacular Banff National Park and Kananaskis Country and bisected by the Trans-Canada Highway, the town of Canmore in Alberta's Bow Valley is a gateway to the scenic splendors of the Canadian Rockies. It's an hour from Calgary and five minutes from Banff National Park, which hosts three to four million visitors each year.

In 1965, some 80 years after Banff became Canada's first national park and Queen Victoria granted the coal mining charter that started Canmore booming, 2,000 people lived there. By the 1970s coal mining had fizzled out and the town's economic future looked grim. Then Canmore was chosen to host the Nordic events at the 1988 Winter Olympics, and the rest, as they say, is history. The town soon became a magnet for outdoor enthusiasts, and by 1993 the population topped 6,000 people. In 2015 there were more than 16,800 full-time and seasonal residents plus thousands of four-season visitors who came from all over the world to play.

The Bow Valley provides an abundance of everything bears are looking for: nutritious natural foods, denning spots, mates, and plenty of room to roam and raise a family. By the 1990s development in Canmore was creating an abundance of unnatural foods for bears. Soon the resident bruins learned it was much easier to pop into town and help themselves to some tasty trash than pick berries all day. Incidents soared and bears were regularly killed for being too good at exploiting this great new food source.

The people of Canmore could have said, "Oh well, that's the price of progress." But they value their wildlife and didn't like the idea of bears being sacrificed so the town could grow and prosper.

In 1997, after studying all the available options, the Waste Management Committee took a deep breath and recommended the town discontinue its traditional curbside trash collection and install 60 big, bear-resistant communal dumpsters instead.

As you can imagine, at first people were reluctant to give up the convenience of curbside. And they worried that the dumpsters would be noisy, ugly, smelly, and a pain in the neck to use. But a survey showed most residents still supported the efforts, because they believed it was up to them to figure out a workable way to coexist with the bears.

For a while the town let people choose between curbside pickup and the community dumpster; by the end of the summer more than half of all households were using community dumpsters. The biggest complaints were from people who wanted the containers closer to their homes. Meanwhile the town was paying double for trash services. You can read all about this interesting exercise in social market-

ing in the Canmore case study from the first edition of *Living With Bears* on my website.

The summer of 1998 saw a widespread failure of natural food sources for bears, and by fall they'd had 300 bear sightings in town, nine bears had been relocated, and four bears had been killed. Citizens got behind the campaign to totally eliminate curbside pickup.

Meanwhile the town figured out that if everyone started using the new system, they'd need a lot more dumpsters. So they doubled the number of dumpsters, and in May of 1999 when they dropped curbside pickup altogether, the bear gravy train came to an abrupt end.

The good news: the number of incidents and problems involving bears in town dropped to zero. And standardizing centralized collection cut the town's trash collection costs by 44 percent and saved the taxpayers a bundle.

The bad news: the bears proved to be even more adaptable than the humans, and started investigating other sources of unnatural foods like bird feeders and compost piles. They also spread out in search of more easy pickings, and soon neighboring towns were experiencing problems.

In 2001 Canmore banned the use of bird feeders from April to October, and the outdoor composting of kitchen waste. With all the preventative measures in place the number of bear incidents plummeted, as did the number of bears destroyed.

One by one the neighboring towns adopted bear-proofing measures as well, and today the Bow Valley is known the world-over for its enlightened and effective waste management programs. In fact, they are doing such a good job of managing garbage, they're working on other programs that include aversive conditioning, removing natural attractants close to town, discouraging or banning the planting of ornamental fruit trees and fruit-bearing bushes, and creating prescriptions for the abundant wildlife corridors that take into consideration both human and wildlife use. For more information, see the Bow Valley WildSmart website: *www.wildsmart.ca*. ❖

14

Protecting Gardens, Orchards and Livestock

Sustainable living is trending, as social media experts would say. People are looking for ways to feel more connected to the earth, and more in control of their food and their environment. Many sound practices like reducing fossil fuel consumption and recycling have grown out of the sustainable living movement. But the more recent trends of growing and raising what you eat, planting edible landscaping and fruit- and nut-bearing trees in neighborhoods, and planting large-scale community gardens all have the potential to create big problems for bears.

Back in the beginning of the 20th century people weren't worried about depleting our natural resources or protecting our wildlife. When animals ate crops, bothered livestock or otherwise got in the way of progress, populations of many species were decimated or totally wiped out. It took more than a century for many populations to recover.

© Sara Tuttle

It's up to us to make sure that cycle of wanton destruction is never set in motion again, so that a century from now writers aren't pointing out how irresponsible and selfish we were "back then." With some thought and effort, you can raise animals, be a bear-responsible gardener, and set a great example for your kids and neighbors.

GARDENS AND FARMS

To a black bear, a garden is just a highly convenient collection of things that are good to eat. Bears love tomatoes, squash, melons, berries, early vegetables, sweet corn—especially when it hits the milk stage—and just about anything else you can grow.

Browse through any popular gardening catalog and it's easy to see that outwitting all the critters that want to eat our gardens is a daunting task. But few catalogs talk about how to safely grow things in bear country. Or caution that some popular critter-repellents like pepper-based deer deterrents and additives like blood meal and fish fertilizer smell like food to a hungry bear.

Tips for Planting a Bear Smart Garden

Plan It. Locate your garden away from your home, and as far away as possible from natural cover and food sources.

Fence It. If your zoning and/or covenants permit, installing an electric fence is a highly effective way to keep bears at bay. Many types of fences are available, including portable and solar models; check out Chapter 15 for more information on choosing and installing an electric fence. If zoning does not permit fencing, consider installing a chain-link pen with a chain-link roof. That will let in the sun and keep out bears (and lots of other critters), as long as they can't dig underneath it.

Pick It. Pick your produce as it ripens. Gardening books recommend you pick in the morning for peak freshness, but leaving ripe produce in the garden overnight is asking for a bear to beat you to it.

Flower gardens are not as attractive to bears as fruit and vegetable gardens, as long as they are not full of dandelions, sweet vetch and clover.

FRUIT TREES & ORCHARDS

Wandering out into the backyard to pick your fill of fruit right off the tree has a lot of nostalgic appeal for people longing to reconnect with simpler times. Unfortunately it also has a lot of practical appeal to bears looking for any shortcut they can find to hitting their calorie quota for the year. Why roam over many miles hunting for native fruits and berries when you can collect all you can possibly eat every day in just an hour or two?

We humans think of fruit as a low calorie, good-for-you-treat, but bears don't eat fruit by the piece. A dozen big ripe apples have more than 1,000 calories. Most fruits are loaded with natural sugars; ingesting a lot of sugar during the late summer and fall gives a bear the energy boost it needs to spend 20 hours a day foraging for food. An orchard filled with ripe fruit is a bear candy store.

Any bears nearby are sure to follow their noses and show up around picking season. If you can't or don't want to fence your orchard, "Please Don't Pick the Fruit" signs won't help; your only practical defense is beating the bears to the bounty. That means pick-

An orchard full of apples is more temptation than a bear can resist. *National Park Service*

ing your fruit all at one time, before it starts to ripen enough to smell, and picking up and removing any fruit that falls to the ground at the end of every day.

Don't dump fallen or buggy fruit near your orchard; it will just attract a variety of wildlife you don't want around, including elk, deer, coyotes, skunks, raccoons and orioles, as well as bears. Leaving it where it falls is like rolling out the red carpet and turning on a big neon "Forage Here" sign for the local wildlife.

Fruit continues to ripen after picking; in fact, most pear varieties won't ripen on the tree; they need to be picked and stored to finish the process. Store your fruit in a cool, bear-proof place.

Pick It Quick or Lose It

"We have about eight acres of wild plums on our property. It was Wednesday when I noticed they were ready to pick, but I was really busy. So we planned to pick everything Saturday, but by then three bears had come through, and there wasn't a single plum left on those trees. I'm glad the bears got a good meal, but we learned our lesson. Pick 'em early if you want to keep them. With plums, it's better to pick them before they're ripe anyway. They have more pectin then, and make better jam," says Melanie Hannafious, who works at Ranch-Way Feeds in northern Colorado.

When he retired from active bear management, Tom Beck established a small organic orchard on his property. He says, "You need to pick all the fruit, and I do mean all; if you leave any fruit up in those hard-to-reach higher branches, the bears will damage or even knock down the tree trying to get at it. With my nectarines, I notice very little wildlife damage until the day I can smell the first fruit. By the next day I can have 25 to 30 percent damage. My biggest culprits are wasps, followed by birds, grey fox and raccoons. So pick early, and save yourself a lot of headaches."

Bear biologists must like growing things, because bear researcher and author Steve Herrero tells this tale in his book, *Bear Attacks: Their Causes and Avoidance.* "I once picked almost the entire crop from our favorite prune-plum tree. The fruit left was at the ends of the highest branches and was the hardest to pick. We put boards with nails sticking outward all around the trunk of the tree and on the major limbs and left for a few days. When we returned, the 20-year-old prune-plum lay on the ground in a heap of broken branches and limbs. Apparently the bear had not been able to reach the fruit without knocking the tree down. Since then I've tried to pick all ripe fruit before leaving."

Think Green When Composting

Grasses, leaves and vegetation should be the only things going into your compost pile when bears are not hibernating. Keep your pile aerated and turned. An occasional sprinkle with lime will help mask odors and speed up the composting process. **Don't put fruit, kitchen waste, meats, dairy, oils, melon rinds or anything else with an odor in your compost pile.** One gardener reported that she'd never had a problem with her compost until the night she added eggshells. The next morning her compost pile was strewn from one end of her yard to the other.

Indoor composting has become a realistic option. Today there are many ingenious indoor composters that are odor-free and easy to use for kitchen scraps. Some of them are so nicely designed they can sit out on your counter. Others are big enough to put in the basement or garage.

RAISING LIVESTOCK IN BEAR COUNTRY

Large-scale commercial ranchers and farmers are usually well-acquainted with everything in their area that poses a danger to their crops, flocks and herds. Enlightened ranchers and farmers work with wildlife managers to remove attractants and minimize risk to both their livelihood and the local wildlife.

But smaller hobby farmers often have no clue what they're getting into when they decide it would be fun to raise a few chickens, become a beekeeper, or fulfill a life-long desire to make their own goat cheese or raise their own pork chops.

Chickens: The New Garbage for Bears

I never realized keeping chickens created such enormous problems for wildlife—not to mention the chickens—until I was on a panel at the 4th International Human Bear Conflicts Workshop in Montana in 2012. In some parts of the country, domestic chickens have replaced garbage as the number one bear attractant.

Americans aren't emotionally attached to their trash, but they love their chickens. Chickens have become symbols of the grow-your-own-food, eat local, get-back-to-your-roots sustainable living movement. There are more than a dozen magazines devoted to backyard chickens. But few people have given much thought to the realities of raising chickens in bear, coyote, skunk, raccoon, snake, bobcat, mountain lion, fox, and birds of prey country. (I'm sure I'm leaving out some species. Unless you're an insect, chickens are pretty much at the bottom of the food chain.) Unprotected chickens, eggs and feed are easy pickings for a wide range of predators, including bears.

And because chickens may be regarded as livestock, wildlife agencies are often legally obligated to let homeowners "defend their chickens," even if that means killing a bear. There's nothing sustainable about that.

"Five years ago all we talked about was garbage, garbage, garbage," said bear biologist Jamie Jonkel, a manager with the Montana Department of Fish, Wildlife and Parks. "Now it's chickens, chickens, chickens."

"More bears were killed over chickens in 2012 than anything else," said Jessica Coltrane, a wildlife biologist with Alaska Fish and Game. "A lot of people having problems were first-time chicken owners."

Or as Grizzly Bear Recovery Coordinator Chris Servheen, who led the successful decades-long effort to restore the then-endangered grizzly bear to the northern Rockies, said, "Does it make sense to kill a grizzly because of a 25-cent chicken?"

"A bear break-in at a chicken coop becomes a cascading event," Servheen explained. "The original chicken owner may fix their problem by putting in an electric fence, but the bear carries that knowledge. They may fix the chicken coop, but we will never fix that bear."

Save Your Chickens

Chickens are pretty defenseless. Letting them roam around on their own is inviting something to come and eat them.

Wildlife predation on chickens is preventable. A sturdy coop and an electric fence around your chicken yard will keep out all manner of things that want to dine on your feathered friends. I asked Colorado District Wildlife Manager Aimee Ryel if she had an electric fence success story I could share and she said "They're all success stories. Bears and electricity just don't mix."

An electric fence will exclude bears, but other critters that like chicken and egg dinners can easily fly or leap over a fence so it's important to remember that your yard needs to have a "lid" as well. Fences should be anchored underground to discourage digging coyotes, foxes and raccoons, usually the first predators to arrive at the coop. See Chapter 15 for more info on electric fences and other deterrents.

Electric fencing keeps chickens in and bears out. *© Bear Smart Durango*

Do the Math

According to *www.poultrykeeper.com*, in the first 18 months of its life, an exceptional hen could lay up to 250 eggs. At a price of $2 a dozen, that's $42 worth of eggs. Multiply by five chickens and that's about $210. If you spend $250 building and fencing a coop, that's four years before you break even on your initial investment, and that doesn't count labor or continuing costs for feed. Or take into consideration the egg-laying lifespan of your average hen, which is somewhere around three or four years for backyard chickens. Just in case you think you are saving money.

What's Eating Your Livestock?

Bears are very opportunistic, and will enthusiastically scavenge another predator's leftovers, or make a meal of an animal that has died of natural causes. Coming across a bear eating a sheep carcass does not mean the bear killed the sheep. It takes a forensic examination of the carcass itself and the inside of the hide, including bite or claw marks and other injuries or wound patterns, to determine how the animal died. If you have an animal that died a suspicious death, don't jump to conclusions. Call your local wildlife agency and ask if someone can come out and determine cause of death.

Predator Pets

Before you blame a bear for a livestock loss, consider this: the most vicious killers of livestock are domestic and feral dogs and cats.

Scientists from the Smithsonian Conservation Biology Institute and the Fish and Wildlife Service used local surveys and pilot studies to estimate the damage done by domestic and feral cats in the United States. Analysis showed that cats kill an astonishing 2.4 billion birds and 12.3 billion mammals every year. That makes the domestic cat one of the single greatest threats to wildlife in the nation, more deadly than pesticides, poisons, automobile strikes, collisions with windows, and all other human-connected causes of death. Cats also prey on chickens, rabbits and other small domestic animals as well.

Domestic and feral dogs kill far more livestock than bears do. Dogs usually mutilate prey; damage to the hindquarters and fore and rear flanks is typical. They often roam in packs, and can do a lot of damage once they begin to attack. Free-roaming dogs instinctively give chase, and will often harass animals for hours. In many states dogs that are chasing or attacking wildlife or livestock can be shot on sight without a permit; check with your local authorities. Owners of dogs and cats that kill livestock can usually be sued for damages.

Think your pet could never turn killer? "Pet owners may not control their animals as much as they should because they are unaware of the threat that domestic dogs and cats pose to livestock and wildlife. Even seemingly harmless and friendly animals instinctually harass and kill wild species and livestock and it's important for members of human communities to understand the real danger of domestic pets running wild," points out APHIS, the U.S. Animal and Plant Health Inspection Service.

THE BUZZ ABOUT BEES

As every Winnie the Pooh fan knows, bears love honey. They also love larval bees, a great source of protein. In fact, it would be tough to

What was left of one of Virginia beekeeper Jay Bradshaw's hives the morning after a bear visit. The bear left some honeycomb behind when it clawed the frame to get at the developing bees. *© Jay Bradshaw*

After bear visits three nights in a row, Jay installed an electric fence. He's had no problems since, and now talks to fellow beekeepers about protecting their hives and the bears. *© Jay Bradshaw*

find a better bear food than a beehive full of honey and brood. Bees are muscle-building protein. Honey is a highly concentrated source of energy. Beehives are especially attractive in the spring before green up and in the fall when bears are non-stop eating machines.

Keeping bees in bear country requires careful planning. Grouping hives closely together makes apiaries easier to manage and protect. Surrounding the apiary with an electric fence is your best defense against bears. A properly maintained electric fence is as close to a bear-proof solution as you'll find, and will eliminate just about all bear damage. Today there are a wide variety of portable and solar-powered fences to choose from. Hives should be at least three feet away from the fence, so a long-armed bear can't simply reach through and knock them down. See Chapter 15 for more on electric fencing.

Constructing an elevated platform is another option. The platform needs to be at least eight feet off the ground with a minimum two-foot overhang, with nothing a bear could climb nearby. Platforms are expensive to build, very hard to move, and if a bear does manage to get up there, it will probably do maximum damage by tossing the bee boxes off the platform onto the ground.

Placement of your beehives can also help prevent bears and other predators from visiting. Beekeepers are looking for locations with dappled sunlight, but hives that are out in the open and at least 300 feet from the forest or other cover are much less attractive to bears. ❖

Community Coexistence at Hemlock Farms

In the busy summer season more than 10,000 residents of the Hemlock Farms community share about eight square miles of Pennsylvania paradise with about 20 resident black bears; that's 2.5 bears per square mile. When you consider those square miles also include more than 3,000 homes, the community's more than 30 years of mostly peaceful coexistence with the bears is even more impressive.

"Most members enjoy and respect the bears, and are careful not to attract them. They've heard too much about the consequences for people and bears if they do," says community manager Mike Sibio, who has been working for Hemlock Farms since 1985.

As always, the biggest challenge remains keeping new members

© Gary Alt

informed about their role in preventing conflicts with the bears, and making sure they understand that feeding bears or deer is not permitted. New residents get a welcome package, and neighbors go out of their way to let them know the community is serious about keeping the peace.

This mama bear is the great granddaughter of a bear Gary Alt nicknamed Vanessa, who raised 28 cubs in 10 years at Hemlock Farms. Her great granddaughter, emerging from her den with cubs, is carrying on the family tradition. *© Gary Alt*

From time to time people break the rules and attract bears, and on a few occasions bears that have made themselves at home in people's homes have had to be killed. But all in all the community has an admirable track record and an even better attitude.

"Not getting along with the bears is not an option," says Sibio. "Bears are so well adapted, that a community in their home range doesn't faze them. It's up to people to accept the fact that bears live in close proximity and we need to educate ourselves on the do's and don'ts of living with them."

Pennsylvania passed an anti-feeding law in 2003. Hemlock Farms has regulations prohibiting feeding, requiring secure bear-resistant containers, and using ammonia in cans on collection day. ❖

"Bears are often needlessly killed, not for what they have done, but for what people think they might do. Many people unjustifiably fear bears, and still believe they cannot survive where humans exist. That is a fallacy," says Gary Alt, Pennsylvania's bear biologist for more than 30 years, who worked closely with Hemlock Farms.

15

Bear Barriers and Deterrents

"Bears aren't on a mission to make your life miserable. They don't know about the time or money you invest in things. They only know there's food and they'd like to have some. So if you live in bear country, you don't have the luxury of waiting until your first bear visit. You have to prevent conflicts from happening in the first place." – Rich Beausoleil

ELECTRIFYING SOLUTIONS

Ordinary fences won't keep out bears. It's easy for a bear to climb up and over to get to something it wants on the other side. Black bears are excellent diggers and can tunnel underneath as well.

A properly constructed, installed, and maintained electric fence is one of the most fool-proof and powerful bear-deterrents available. Farm and ranch stores and most home improvement stores offer affordable and effective portable and permanent electric fencing.

Bears and electricity just don't mix. When a bear's super-sensitive lips, nose or tongue come in contact with 6,000 volts, the bear has an experience it never wants to repeat. Getting shocked does no permanent damage, but it makes a permanent and lasting impression. And best of all it prevents the bear from getting a food reward.

Advances in solar technology and battery capabilities mean that electricity can now be used in ways that weren't feasible even 20 years ago. Today there are permanent fencing systems powerful enough to successfully keep grizzly bears out of landfills, campgrounds, or even an entire village. There are portable electric fences that can be set up and functional in less than two hours, and solar-powered systems that can be installed anywhere there's enough sun to charge the batteries. There are even lightweight, battery-powered fences that weigh less than four pounds and cost under $300 that can protect a 30-foot x 30-foot campsite. Clever people have electrified everything from doormats and coolers to horse trailers and refrigerators.

Twenty-five states and many Canadian provinces either loan fences or provide funding; many also provide on-site advice and hands-on assistance. For a list of guides, resources and more information about electric deterrents, see the resources section at *www.LivingWithBears.com*.

How An Electric Fence Works

An electric fence acts like an open circuit, with repeating pulses of electricity produced by the energizer flowing through the charged wires of the fence. When something touches a charged wire, it grounds the fence, creating a closed circuit—and a shocking encounter.

Voltage and Joules

Bears have heavy fur, very thick skin, a high tolerance for pain, and heavy foot pads that minimize grounding. Because they have big thick fur coats and insulating layers of fat, experts recommend a minimum of 6,000 volts to effectively shock a black bear. But it's the joules rating on your energizer that tells you the amount of energy your fence actually delivers. You need at least 0.7 joules delivered, depending on your local moisture conditions. Enough is good; more is not better. The higher the joule output, the greater the danger to humans or pets that accidentally come into contact.

Permanent Electric Fencing

Once properly installed, a permanent electric fence can be left in place for years. Permanent fences stand up under environmental stresses like snowloads better than portable fences. You can also tighten high-tensile wire to 200 psi, so that when a bear pushes against the wire, the tension separates the bear's fur, allowing the wire to deliver a shock right to the skin. In the long run, installing a permanent electric fence can be the most cost-effective and foolproof way of keeping bears out of places people don't want bears to be.

Minimum Electric Fence Specs for Deterring Bears

Joules	0.7 delivered
Voltage	6,000 or more
Fence Height	4 feet or more
Wires	5 or more

Portable Electric Fences

Portable electric fences can be a good solution for areas and situations where a permanent fence is impractical. A 30- x 42-foot temporary fence can hold 32 bee colonies or protect a small grove of fruit trees or a camper parked off the beaten path. There are even fences that can be used in areas without good grounding, like sand or dry gravel.

Conflicts prevention expert Patti Sowka shows how portable solar panels let you install an electric fence anywhere there's sun. *© Patti Sowka*

Maintenance Is Key

Anything that comes in contact with a charged wire can create a partially or completely closed circuit, including fallen tree branches, blowing vegetation, or other animals like raccoons or deer. Routine maintenance is the key to keeping an electric fence in top shape; if a downed tree branch closes a circuit, the fence is powerless until the branch is removed and the circuit is open again. For the best performance, somebody should inspect the fence line every day or two.

- Grass or shrubs touching the wires draw down voltage; keep grass cut low under the bottom wire.
- Keep wires tight and batteries charged. DC fence chargers (6- and 12-volt) need their batteries recharged every two to four weeks.
- Use at least a 70 amp-hour battery.
- The fence charger should always be on. Check voltage weekly with a voltmeter. You should have at least 3,000 volts at the furthest distance from the charger. Always recharge during the day, so the fence is at maximum output at night, when bears are most likely to come calling.
- Marine battery terminals and lead-composition eyelets resist corrosion. Keep your battery and fence charger dry and corrosion free. Disconnect lower wires if they're covered by snow.
- Gates should be electrified, well-insulated, and practical—they can range from single strands of electrified wire with gate handles to electrified panels or tubular gates.

Safe, Not Sorry

Electric fencing combines high voltage with low amperage in a pulsating charge at 60–65 pulses a minute. Breaking the circuit and getting shocked creates an involuntary muscle contraction. The pulsating charge gives the person (or bear) a fraction of a second to let go of the wire.

Whatever you do, don't make the mistake one of our neighbors did and wire straight into the household current instead of using a fence charger. Households use continuous alternating current (AC) and it is always on. Plug into an outlet and when something or someone gets zapped their muscles will contract and only partially release—making it hard to let go, and easy to get hurt.

Getting zapped by an electric fence doesn't do any permanent damage to bears or people. But it's highly unpleasant, so put up a warning sign. In some areas, electric fences are not permitted within city or township limits. Check with your homeowners association or local government before installing one.

Electric Fencing

"An electric fence is 100 percent effective at deterring both grizzly and black bears if it is maintained properly," says Mark Bruscino, long-time supervisor of the Wyoming Department of Game and Fish's large carnivore program. Wyoming DGF installs permanent electric fences in areas where bears are continually testing their human neighbors. Bruscino estimates that bears have challenged one particular Gallagher USA electric fence encircling a campground hundreds of times without breaking through. "Usually they just spin around and take off," he says.

UNWELCOME MATS

Bear unwelcome mats are designed to provide a barrier that keeps bears out. They can be conventional or electric. Properly constructed, installed and maintained, they cause instant pain if a bear attempts to walk over the mat to reach a door or window, but do no permanent damage.

Unwelcome mats can be left in place underneath windows or seldom-used doors, or put in place when you'll be away from home. They can be used anywhere as a temporary, short-term measure to deter a specific bear from returning.

Conventional unwelcome mats meant to deter black bears are usually made of sheets of sturdy plywood that have been carefully studded with small nails pointing up. Nails should be long enough to stick out of the wood ¾ to 1 inch and set approximately 2 inches apart. Place the mat nail-side up in front of bear-accessible windows and doors. As long as it's big enough to keep a bear from reaching over or around them, an unwelcome mat is very effective. The mat should extend past the sides of the door or window a minimum of two feet. A 4x4 sheet of plywood will protect a single doorway; a 4x8 sheet will protect most patio and double doors and windows.

Unwelcome mats were invented by Alaskans to deter grizzly bears. Grizzlies have bigger feet, longer claws and heavier paw pads than black bears. A mat designed for a grizzly can easily cripple a black bear, so make sure you follow the specification for the species you're out to deter.

How To Install an Unwelcome Mat

The mat needs to be big enough to fully cover the entire area in front of the doors or windows where the bear is trying to gain entry. If it's on a deck, screw or tack it down so the bear can't shove it out of the way.

If it's on the ground, pound two 18-inch sections of rebar in each outer corner, or drill holes in the front two corners and pound in long spikes with sturdy heads. Your objective is to "nail down" the mat so the bear can't move it. You'll find illustrated fact sheets and detailed design and installation instructions at *www.LivingWithBears.com.*

Electric Unwelcome Mats

You can make an electric unwelcome mat in a couple of hours from easily available materials. When a bear steps on the mat, it gets shocked. Humans or pets coming into contact with the mat could also get a brief shock. While it's uncomfortable, it's not harmful and certainly not lethal. As with all electrifying solutions, mats must be properly constructed, installed, and maintained to be effective.

This ingenious electric unwelcome mat was the brainchild of Colorado District Wildlife Manager Kevin Wright. See *www.LivingWithBears.com* for instructions.

OTHER DETERRENTS

Bears don't like surprises, and often flee things that startle them. Adult black bears have been observed climbing trees to get away from great blue herons. (No, a plastic heron planted in your yard will not deter a bear.) Just be aware that many of these devices may fool an individual bear once or twice, but eventually it may learn that your flashing scarecrow is harmless.

Motion-Activated Lights, Sirens, Sprinklers

Motion-activated lights, loud sirens, and sprinklers may temporarily deter a bear, but if nothing else happens to reinforce the experience, there's evidence the bear will eventually learn to ignore them. The lights and noisemakers can alert you that something is in your yard, and give you time to take action, but they are not a substitute for thoroughly bear-proofing your place or installing a more permanent deterrent, like an electric fence.

Other Noisemakers

Air horns, whistles and other loud, high-pitched noisemakers may hurt a bear's ears and startle it enough to chase it off, and because they make sounds not heard in nature, bears are not sure how to react. Air horns can be found in handy travel sizes (great for hiking); countertop models from the boating supplies section of discount and sporting goods stores will cost less than ten bucks.

Radios and TVs

The unexpected sound of the human voice can startle a bear enough to cause it to leave the area. If you are going to be gone for an extended period of time, you can leave a radio or TV on a timer. Just be sure it's tuned in to a talk station. If the host is loud and cantankerous and given to explosive blasts of commentary, all the better.

One of our neighbors installed a "guard radio" inside her chicken coop in an attempt to deter a bear that had been nosing around the neighborhood and managed to reach in through an open coop door and help itself to dinner. Apparently bears are not attracted to Fox News, as the broadcasts kept the bear at a safe distance from the coop. The chickens' owner found bear scat in the area, but there was no further bear damage or missing chickens. And it didn't seem to bother the birds any. They kept on laying eggs right on schedule. An electric fence and a sturdy roofed enclosure would be an even better idea. See Chapter 14 for more about raising livestock in bear country.

Barking Dog Alarm

A barking dog may convince a bear to move on. Just be sure your dog is secured; dogs chasing bears in people's backyards are often injured, or lead the bear back to their owner. Turn on the lights and survey the yard before letting your dog out at night. If you spot a bear, let your dog bark, but don't turn it loose. Don't have a dog? Rex Plus is an electronic watchdog that's about the size of a small stereo speaker. Rex can detect motion through doors, walls, and windows up to 30 feet away. Add a Guard Dog on Duty sign and put a pet bowl on the porch and human intruders may also be persuaded to give your place a wide berth. Rex is made by Safety Technology International.

Ammonia and Bleach

A bear's nose is 2,100 times more sensitive than yours. So if a good sniff of bleach makes your eyes water, imagine what it might do to a bear's.

Used separately, straight ammonia or bleach is a powerful irritant best used to create an odor barrier, not as a weapon. An ammonia bath is a great way to disinfect garbage cans, scrub down barbeque grills, or spray down tents. Some people report success with buckets of sponges soaked in ammonia, bleach, or a strong cleaner like Lysol or Pine Sol. Refresh often, and don't use anything lemon or pleasantly scented; these types of odors can actually act as an attractant.

Don't use ammonia or bleach in a squirt gun or a water balloon that may burst under pressure and splash up into a bear's eyes. A good dose of ammonia or bleach can permanently injure or even blind a bear.

Never combine ammonia and bleach; you will create a potentially fatal concoction that can cause your lungs to fill with liquid instead of air.

Bear Spray Isn't a Repellent

Bear spray has an excellent track record for deterring bears (Chapter 23), so naturally some people have tried to use it as a preventative measure, spraying down tents, sleeping bags and camp perimeters. In addition to being very expensive, using bear spray as a repellent is highly ineffective. In fact, there's evidence that once the oily, pepper-based spray dries, the odor that clings to everything actually attracts bears and other animals.

Black bears were attracted to bear spray residue in Great Smoky Mountains National Park, according to results from a science project and field study done in 2010 by 8th grader Baylee Stiver, whose dad Bill is the Park's Supervisory Wildlife Biologist. Her motion-detector cameras captured several bears, along with deer, squirrels, wild turkeys and a coyote, sniffing repeatedly at the residue.

Actions Speak Lots Louder Than Words

Unfortunately, simply believing that people have a real responsibility to do their part to prevent problems for bears and their fellow humans isn't enough. We must find ways to motivate ourselves, our neighbors and our communities to act on those beliefs.

It's sobering to realize that something that seems so inconsequential—putting the trash out at night, feeding the birds, or forgetting to bring in the dog food, pick your produce or lock up the chickens—can start a chain of events that ends in death.

So ask yourself what you're willing to do to break that chain. Would you invest in a bear-resistant container? Get up in time to take the trash out the morning of pickup instead of the night before? Put away your bird feeders and find other ways to attract your feathered friends? Spend an afternoon picking ripened fruit? Protect your chickens, beehives or gardens with an electric fence?

If you're reading this, I hope your answer is yes. Yes is the price we need to be willing to pay for living where bears are trying to make a home too. ❖

Playing Smart in Bear Country

© Tom Rogers, Vermont Fish & Wildlife

16

On the Trail

When the first settlers arrived in North America, they had little choice but to make their way into the wilderness. Today someone could theoretically live their entire life in the concrete jungle, never more than a few minutes away from all the comforts civilization has to offer.

And yet millions of people spend much of their precious free time trying to escape from the civilization we created and get back to that wild world that still exists beyond the parking lot.

Ask why and people shake their heads and look at you in bewilderment. If you have to ask, you just don't get it.

Recreation in what is left of the great outdoors is booming, driven by the growing popularity of pastimes like mountain biking, orienteering, rock climbing, geocaching, and mushroom-hunting plus a resurgence of interest in old standbys like hiking, camping, fishing, horseback riding, photography, and bird watching.

Whether you're taking your dog for a walk in the greenbelt, looking for a quiet place to picnic, camping with the family, or backpacking into the wilderness, when you step off the pavement, you need to start playing by Mother Nature's rules if you want to get along with the natives.

Just Out For a Walk

Most hikers who end up lost for days were just out for a day hike. They weren't prepared for anything to go wrong. They weren't dressed properly; they didn't have enough food and water; they often left without maps or compasses or emergency supplies or even telling anyone where they were going.

Many people who encounter bears in developed areas in parks and along walking paths and bike trails are equally unprepared. If you're recreating in known bear habitat, you should realize there's a reasonable chance you could run into a bear, and know how to respond if you do.

Dog Walking in Bear Country

Many people think that walking with their dog provides extra protection. Manitoba bear biologist Hank Hristienko and researcher Steve Herrero's recent research shows that just the opposite may usually be the case. Between 2010 and 2014 there were 92 reports of black bears attacking humans across North America. Dogs were involved in more than half (53 percent) of the instances. Eighteen dogs were injured and seven were killed by the bear involved.

If you hike with dogs, they should be on leash and under control at all times.

From the reports, the authors surmised that the vast majority of the dogs involved had been off leash at the time of the attack, and most likely drew the bear back to their owner. Of those 92 total attacks, 23 involved a female bear with cubs. Looking just at those instances, dogs were involved in 21 out of the 23 attacks. Of the three human fatalities during that same time period, one involved an individual who'd let his dog out for a walk.

Ongoing research clearly shows that female black bears very seldom attack people to defend their cubs, although they may fight back if provoked or harassed by people or dogs. Evidently mother bears consider a dog snapping and barking at their offspring as harassment.

When species share space, competition often develops. Wolves, foxes, coyotes, bobcats, mountain lions, eagles, and even other bears are known to kill black bear cubs. Hristienko and Herrero suggest that bears react to dogs as if they were threatening competitors, and sometimes attack or kill them. In areas where dogs are used to hunt bears, the local ursine population may have a canine chip on its collective shoulders. And person plus dog may be more alarming to a bear than either one by itself and could trigger a defensive reaction.

The *Alaska Dispatch News* reported that 57-year-old Alaskan hiker Thea Thomas was hiking along a wilderness trail near a stream filled with spawning salmon when one of two dogs she had with her ran ahead—and soon sprinted back, chased by a brown bear. "The dog just kept running," Thomas said. "The bear stopped and started swatting me. For a while I thought I was going to die." Despite being bitten several times, she managed to walk more than a mile back to her car and drive herself to the hospital. It was the first time in her 30 years of hiking she'd encountered an angry bear.

Experts recommend that if you're going to walk your dog in bear country, you should keep your dog on a short leash at all times; under voice command is not enough. Letting it roam around so it can scare up any bears in the area that were trying to avoid you can be downright dangerous. It's a good idea to carry bear spray. A sturdy walking stick can also come in handy. Don't talk on the phone or listen to music; pay attention to your surroundings, and familiarize yourself with the tips for hiking in bear country and avoiding confrontations and surprises that can be unnerving for people, dogs and bears.

© Mark Gocke

HIKING IN BEAR COUNTRY

Most people who love the outdoors are drawn to wild places. My husband and I have worn out countless pairs of hiking boots in our many years of trekking through places bears call home. For us, not knowing what's around the next bend in the trail or what's making that mysterious rustling in the bushes is part of the adventure. We realize there's a chance of getting stung or bitten or twisting an ankle trying to rock-hop across a stream. There's even a slim possibility we could have a scary encounter with wildlife that could hurt us.

But there's also a chance we could see a spotted fawn frolicking in a wildflower-filled meadow, listen to the bugling of a bull elk in rut, spot a golden eagle soaring overhead or, if we're very lucky, watch a black bear industriously digging grubs out of a rotting log.

For us the potential rewards far outweigh the potential risks. But that's a personal decision every hiker has to make for themself. We're much more worried about encounters with crazy drivers on the way to the trailhead than wayward wildlife. You have to come to terms with that slight element of danger if you're going to spend time in the woods. As elsewhere in life, there are no guarantees.

What Do We Do When We See a Bear?

We think it's our lucky day when we spot a bear. Over the years we've been fortunate enough to see many black bears, and a few elusive grizzlies. Sometimes we've been able to sit and watch a bear through our binoculars without bothering it. Other times we've simply gone our separate ways; we knew the bear was there, and the bear knew we were there, and we mutually agreed to avoid each other. And even though we've never come close to having an aggressive bear encounter out day hiking, we never leave the trailhead without our bear spray. See Chapter 21 for more on encountering bears.

© Tim Halvorson

Not Orphaned Cubs

Many states have programs designed to care for orphaned bear cubs in ways that allow them to be returned to the wild when they are old enough to fend for themselves. These popular programs generate maximum warm fuzzies with the public, but many of the cubs that end up in rehab weren't really orphans. If a den is disturbed, a mother bear will often run away from the site, but she usually doesn't run very far. She's often hovering a few hundred yards away, waiting for the people to go away so she can return to her offspring. If you find a young cub, leave the area and give mom plenty of time to come back. If you return the next day to a bawling and miserable little bear, then you can call in the cavalry.

Before You Go

If you're visiting an area for the first time, get bear smart before you go. Find out whether there are black bears, grizzly bears or both, and if there have been any recent problems. Familiarize yourself with local conditions and regulations. If you arrive at a trailhead or campground and see "Bear Frequenting the Area" signs, bear-resistant storage lockers, or other evidence that bears are regular visitors, take extra precautions, for your sake and the bears'.

In many places with high numbers of both people and bears, the resident bruins have learned that ice chests, bags and boxes contain nutritious food surprises. Oftentimes there are regulations prohibiting leaving food or anything else that might attract a bear's attention in your vehicle overnight. Ignoring them can result in hefty fines, or having your food or vehicle impounded.

And getting fined will be the least of your problems if a determined bear discovers goodies in your car. In many locales bears have learned to open car door handles or resort to simpler tricks, like bashing out a window, to get their paws on food inside.

Even if there are no mandatory food storage regulations, don't leave things like coolers, grocery sacks, food, beverages, trash or empty cans, bottles or packages where a bear could see or smell them. Lock attractants in your trunk or a secure storage container you can cover with a dark blanket.

Delaware North at Yosemite

Bears are attracted to just about anything that smells, from dirty diapers to lemon-scented cleaners. Wildlife officers use vanilla air freshener to bait live traps. Safely store your scented toiletries, soaps, sunscreens and anything else with an odor with your food.

Bear-Resistant Storage Lockers

Two Adirondack Park campgrounds in New York, Limekiln Lake and Forked Lake, went from most problematic to least problematic after installing bear-resistant storage lockers. Such lockers are widely used in places that have a history of chronic problems with bears helping themselves to easily accessible human food, like California's Yosemite National Park. Bear-resistant storage lockers virtually eliminate problems with bears as long as there are enough lockers to handle peak demand and family groups and people understand why and how to use them. Using a bear-resistant storage locker will protect both your food and the bears.

When On the Trail

If you absolutely, positively DON'T want to see a bear there are some precautions you can take that will reduce your odds of a sighting or encounter.

Read the Signs. Numerous studies show that many people have a bad case of sign-blindness. But signage may be the only way authorities can reach out to every passing hiker or camper. Information boards often contain lists of wildlife sightings, trail conditions and other helpful information, like "bridge out 5 miles ahead." Sometimes trails, campgrounds or backcountry campsites are temporarily closed because of bear activity in the area. Take warning signs about bear activity seriously; they are posted so you will know to be extra alert. Ignoring trail closures and cautions puts both you and the bears at risk. If bears could read, posting "People in the Area. Avoid at All Costs" signs would prevent a lot of problems.

Hike Mid-Day. Most wildlife, including bears, are most active

in the early morning, near dusk and at night. If you hike in the middle of the day, most of the wildlife you see will be other hikers.

Hike in Groups. The more the merrier. Lots of people make lots of noise, and wild creatures get plenty of warning they have company coming and generally flee.

Make Noise. Talk loudly, sing and occasionally clap your hands or blow your whistle and you can be pretty sure anything within earshot will most likely avoid you. Most experts do not recommend bear bells. There's no evidence they're effective, and some evidence that some bears have learned to associate the sound with food. Bear bells are also 100-percent certain to annoy your fellow hikers.

Pay Attention. If you're hiking in rough terrain, it's easy to focus on the trail instead of the woods around you, so stop frequently and look around. An extra bonus, you'll enjoy your hike more when you take time to look at something other than the trail beneath your feet.

Watch for Signs of Bear Activity. Watch the trail and surrounding area for fresh scat, tracks, rubbings or other evidence of bears that might be in the area. See Chapter 20 for more information.

Avoid Food Sources and Travel Corridors. Berry patches in the late summer, dense cover, streams, and edge zones where forest meets meadow are common places for wildlife sightings.

Double Bag Your Food. If you're going to be out for several hours and you're packing lunch, snacks, sunscreen, lip balm, and other things with an odor, seal everything in double plastic freezer bags or turkey-roasting bags, and use the empties to pack out your trash. Don't leave so much as an orange peel or apple core behind; you'll teach bears and other critters to associate trails with food.

Eyes on the Skies. Circling scavenger birds often indicate a dead animal—and a good area to avoid. If you come across a fresh or cached carcass, be very alert and leave the area immediately—generally it's safe to go back the way you came, assuming you didn't run into a bear on the way in.

Don't Hike at Night. This may seem painfully obvious, but the popularity of personal headlamps would indicate plenty of people hike in the dark. If you're coming back or heading out after sundown or before dawn, be aware wildlife often use people trails at night. Wild animals don't need headlamps to see in the dark. Black bears blend into the night, and have much better night vision than you do.

Hiking with Dogs. Many people believe that hiking with their dog improves their safety in bear country, but recent research would indicate the opposite is true. See the section on dog walking for more details. National parks in the U.S. prohibit dogs on trails altogether. Regulations vary in Canada, but where dogs are allowed they must be on a short leash at all times.

Hiking with Kids. Kids are notorious for attempting to escape from their parents, whether they're in a shopping mall or in the great outdoors. People who'd never let their children roam through the suburbs alone think nothing of letting them run ahead or lag behind in the woods; an indulgence that can have tragic consequences.

Get in the habit of making a kid sandwich: adults are the bread, kids are the filling. The filling has to stay between the bread at all times. That way if you do encounter wildlife or potentially dangerous conditions, everyone will be together and the grownups will be able to focus on how to respond, instead of worrying about where their children are. Plus the larger the group, the less likely you are to be involved in an aggressive bear encounter. And in the much more likely event that you see something amazing, you'll all be able to share the experience together.

Teach kids not to squeal, shriek or make noises that could make them sound like prey, and not to run under any circumstances. If everyone carries a whistle you'll all have an easy way to sound an alarm.

OTHER DAY-TIME ACTIVITIES

"Pick-a-Nicks"

Like Yogi and Boo Boo, some bears accustomed to sharing space with humans develop a nose for a well-stuffed pick-a-nick basket. When people leave garbage and food scraps behind in popular picnic areas, the local bears often learn to show up and clean up the leftovers. And sometimes they don't wait until you've left.

Don't teach bears to associate picnic grounds with easy food rewards. Pack a spray bottle of cleaner, and wipe down your table before and after you eat. Stay close to your food, don't feed anything that comes begging, and clean up thoroughly when you're done.

Don't leave any food or scraps behind. If there are no bear-resistant trash containers, take your trash with you. If you're cooking, remember that cooking intensifies food odors, and bears can smell

This young bear in Great Smoky Mountains National Park was attracted to apple cores, food, and trash people left along the trail. Eventually it bit a visitor and had to be killed. Pack it in, pack it out, and don't let your leftovers turn into deadly weapons.
© Warren Bielenberg

food from as far as five miles away. Burn food particles off the grill completely; dirty grills and scraps left behind in fire pits encourage bears to come visit.

If you're picnicking off the beaten path, pick an area with a good view of your surroundings and away from dense cover and any natural foods like berries or clover patches. Check for signs of recent bear activity before you settle in, be alert while you're there, and don't leave any trace of your presence behind.

Why Can't We Feed the Bears?

Some people think there's nothing wrong with leaving food out for the bears. For some, waiting for the bears to show up is the evening entertainment. Others want a photo to post on Facebook or an instant celebrity video for YouTube. Some think it's a less wasteful way of taking out the garbage. Others truly seem to think the bears are starving, and donuts and fried chicken will save them.

"The bears are already used to it," you reason. "One more hunk of watermelon won't make any difference. And I want the kids to see a bear." Bears that learn to associate people with food usually lead short and unhappy lives. So unless you want the kids to see a bear being trapped and killed, don't feed the bears.

© Warren Bielenberg

Fringe Benefits

Ground-level fire pits in Great Smoky Mountains National Park were replaced with raised grills to make things easier for picnickers. And they ended up being good for bears. The park discovered that people don't throw trash into the raised grills, so bears no longer dig through looking for treats.

Biking

Bikes are quiet and fast; you can cover a lot of ground in a short time. Riding a bike on trails through parks and wildlands increases the possibility you'll surprise a bear or trick a mountain lion into thinking you are prey zooming by. Bears don't like to be surprised, and may react badly to suddenly finding you on top of them. Bicyclists may be especially vulnerable in areas with roadside bears. Some cyclists attach a can with pebbles to their bike, or add bells or horns, put a playing card in the wheel spokes, or use noisemakers. If you're biking in bear country, it's smart to avoid dawn or dusk rides, and to travel at speeds that allow you to keep an eye on your surroundings. Bike with a friend if you can; you'll make more noise, and have someone available to help in an emergency.

Jogging

Joggers are even more preoccupied with watching the trail than hikers and cyclists, and often jog at dawn and dusk when bears and other wildlife are most active. If you must jog in the early morning or evening, avoid roads and trails that go through dense cover, or where there are frequent bear sightings. It's not safe to zone out in bear country, so leave your smart phone in your pocket and your personal portable sound system at home. If you can, jog with a friend and periodically make some noise—give a nice war whoop, sing a few bars, or blow your whistle. If you are in mountain lion country, be even more alert, as running can trigger a chase response from predators. Tying bear bells into your shoes is both annoying and ineffective.

What to Carry When You Jog or Bike

Carry bear spray in a chest or waist holster along with a safety whistle and/or a small, portable air horn and your cell phone. Tuck an identification card with emergency contact info in your pocket...just in case.

Horseback Riding

Horses, llamas, donkeys and other livestock detect bears before people do, and bears often detect them. Most bears associate livestock with people, and give the whole party a wide berth. According to Steve Herrero's research, no one on horseback has ever been attacked and injured by a bear, although people have been thrown off and injured when their horse sensed a bear was nearby and bolted or bucked. If you're heading out for an overnight pack trip, pack bear spray and hang your stock feed with your food, or store inside a portable electric fence or bear-resistant locker or container.

OFF-TRAIL ACTIVITIES

Geocaching and Orienteering

Geocaching and orienteering are challenging adventure sports that require sophisticated off-trail navigational skills and intense concentration. Unfortunately they can often lead participants deep into relatively unexplored terrain where the odds of encountering a bear unfamiliar with people go up, and the odds of the person being bear aware and prepared for a sighting or encounter go down. You're focused on your objective, not your surroundings. That's a recipe for disaster in the wilderness. Many parks and forests frown on off-trail and cross-country adventures because there are so many things that can go wrong, and it's easy to blunder into sensitive habitat. If you're going off trail, study the rules for hiking safely, be aware of seasonal area closures, and make sure you know how to respond to and deal with all types of bear and wildlife encounters.

From Berries to Bird Watching

Virtually any activity that takes you into the woods and requires you to focus intently on something else requires an extra degree of caution and planning in bear country. When you're looking for the perfect morel or the ripest berries, you're not looking for bears. But you are looking for things that bears love to eat. If you're successful in your quest, you'll be carting around a big sack of bear food and you won't be paying attention to what you're doing, where you're going, or what you might be sharing space with. You need to be fully prepared for all the same situations you could encounter hiking or backpacking.

On National Public Lands Day each September volunteers collect and remove an estimated 500 tons of trash from our national parks and other public lands.

KNOW WHEN TO PLAY IT SAFE

We often hike at dawn and dusk, near wildlife corridors like stream beds and meadow edges. Sometimes we'll go an hour or more without uttering a word. That's because one of the reasons we hike is to see wildlife, and you can't have everything. If you follow all the avoidance guidelines, chances are good you won't see any bears, or anything else.

But we don't take unnecessary risks. We follow the rules when circumstances dictate that avoidance is the smart choice. If we're hiking with the wind in our face and the trail twists and turns along a stream bed and in and out of patches of ripe berries, we become very talkative. We stop and clap our hands before we round a bend. Sometimes when the hairs on the backs of our necks stand up and we get that funny feeling, we even turn around.

We also take extra precautions at dawn and dusk and in the late summer and fall, when bears don't think about much of anything except eating 20 hours a day, and are more likely to be so food-absorbed they don't notice you coming. As the long winter's fast draws closer, bears can be less likely to give ground if they've found a good food source. ❖

Common Problems, Uncommon Solutions

"It would be easy to manage the bears. All you'd have to do is keep out the people."

Bill Stiver told me that in 2005 when I was finishing up the first edition of *Living With Bears*. I chuckled, but soon realized he had gotten right to the crux of a universal challenge.

Today Stiver is Great Smoky Mountains National Park's Supervisory Wildlife Biologist, having taken over from the legendary Kim DeLozier in 2011. DeLozier had a well-deserved reputation for being a practical problem solver with an uncanny ability to think like a bear and an unwillingness to take "we can't do that" for an answer. He instilled his "we will find a way" attitude in everyone who worked with him. Maybe that's why there are several Smoky Mountain success stories scattered throughout this book.

Back in 1991when Stiver walked away from a cushy desk job in Oklahoma to join the park he loved as a temporary employee, hundreds of mailbox-style bear-resistant garbage cans were in use. Or more accurately, were in overuse. Capacity was no match for the park's annual nine million-plus visitors' ability to produce trash. The containers were always overflowing, with garbage often left outside. As the day worn on, the more garbage piled up.

They replaced the garbage cans with bear-resistant dumpsters. But the root of the problem was that even though the maintenance crew worked hard emptying dumpsters and picking up after people, they went off duty at 3:30 p.m. By nightfall fire pits were full of food scraps and garbage was piled outside the dumpsters. Popular sites like Chimneys picnic area developed a well-deserved reputation as the place to bring your lawn chairs and snacks and watch the nightly bear show.

The park's wildlife staff made a career out of trapping, working up and relocating bears, with the usual results. They grew weary of the bear relocation assembly line, and started looking for more effective solutions. That search resulted in an innovative approach to problem solving which changed things for the better.

Scheduling the last trash pickup later in the day seemed like it would be a simple solution. But people were being asked to change more than their hours. They were also being asked to change their very culture. Many of the old timers knew that people came to the park hoping to see some bears, and didn't understand what harm there was in making it easy for them.

So the bear folks set about rounding up enough evidence to show why the status quo was bad for bears. For two years a bear squad of biologists, interns, and biotechs cruised the park at night, policing and cleaning up the grounds, taking photos of the trash that had piled up after the crew went off duty, and documenting bears getting into trouble.

Nothing like a ticket to let people know that food storage regulations are enforced.
© Warren Bielenberg

Today they'd take photos on their smart phones and push send, but back then DeLozier brought their Polaroids to the weekly staff meeting and "shared" them with everyone. After two years of "sharing" the maintenance chief agreed something had to change.

So the day shift became the swing shift. They now work from 1:00 p.m. to 9:30 p.m. The park helps out by closing the three most problematic picnic areas at 8:00 in the summer so they can be cleaned up before sundown. These changes solved so many chronic issues with bears that sometimes Stiver has to remind folks why it's important for them to work until 9:30 at night.

The wildlife staff still monitors the picnic areas at night; all that picnicking leaves plenty of odors behind that inevitably attract bears. If they start to see an individual bear on a regular basis, they will capture it, work it up, and release it on-site. ❖

Scenes like this one used to be commonplace in GSMNP and many other parks. *National Park Service*

GSMNP now holds people accountable for the problems they create. *© Warren Bielenberg*

"We want visitors to have the opportunity to safely see and enjoy wildlife, particularly an amazing animal like a black bear. With 1,600 black bears and more than nine million visitors, we are going to have a lot of human-bear interactions. Fortunately efforts by all park staff to keep human food and garbage away from bears, and our efforts to teach bears to avoid people have really cut down on the negative interactions." — *Bill Stiver, Supervisory Wildlife Biologist, Great Smoky Mountains National Park*

17

Camping, Backpacking and Fishing in Bear Country

Many frontcountry campers show up toting enough calories to put the average bear into a food coma. Combine plenty of available food with an endless supply of calorie-laden garbage and it's easy to see why bears are attracted to campgrounds.

Whether you're camping in a drive-to, developed campground, a hike-in backcountry camp, or just pitching your tent in the middle of nowhere, some common-sense precautions can help keep your camp bear-free.

Great Smoky Mountains National Park

Do Your Camping Homework

Tactics that might be more than adequate if you're frontcountry camping in an area where bears are few and far between may prove woefully inadequate—or even illegal—in a region like the Sierra Nevada Mountains where bears excel at filching provisions. Do your homework before you go. Nothing puts a quick end to a camping trip like losing all your supplies to a foraging bear.

When you arrive at your site, take a look around and see if there is any evidence of recent bear activity, like scattered trash or burned bits of who knows what raked out of the fire pit. If there is, it's a good indication that people before you have been sloppy and careless and have taught bears to routinely investigate the site; take photos, contact the authorities and consider camping somewhere else.

Clean Up Your Act

Keep a clean camp. Leaving food, trash or other things with odors in the open is asking for bear trouble. Know and follow local food storage regulations and recommendations. Treat all your scented toiletries and other items as if they were food—bears don't know your coconut sunscreen or peppermint toothpaste isn't good to eat. It's best to avoid heavily scented products altogether.

Don't bury or burn garbage or trash. Burning actually makes trash more attractive, because the food molecules and odors intensify and disperse on the wind. This goes double for burning trash in your fire ring or barbecue grate. Bears will dig through the remains looking for goodies. If bear-resistant garbage cans or dumpsters are available, use them—and properly close and latch them when you're through. Don't leave trash outside. If the container is overflowing or broken, double bag your trash and stash it in your trunk.

Pack a can of Lysol. Or mix up a concoction of 50 percent ammonia and 50 percent water, and spray your picnic table, the outside of your tent, and your backpack or day pack frequently. Don't use bear spray as a repellent; it's designed to deter bears in an encounter. There is some evidence that when bear spray dries, the pepper-based residue may actually attract bears. See Chapter 23 for more.

Make your tent a food-free zone. There are few things more startling than being woken up in the middle of the night by a bear licking the remnants of a chocolate bar off your face. Don't eat in your tent or sleeping bag, and store food and all scented toiletries, including lip balm, as far away from your tent as possible. Food or other attractants have been involved in the vast majority of incidents involving a black bear entering someone's tent.

Store the clothes you cook in along with your food, and wear clean clothes for sleeping. Clean yourself up with unscented soap; there's evidence overly-ripe human smells may attract bears. Don't turn in with so much as a breath mint or a tube of toothpaste in your tent.

Cooking grease, dishwashing liquid, and liquid used to cook or boil food all smell great to a bear. Bring something to collect grease, double bag it, and pack it out. Filter food particles out of the dishwater—use a tea strainer or a small piece of window screening—and store them with your garbage. Dump the remaining dishwashing and cooking liquid well away from and downwind of your sleeping and cooking areas.

Burn off any food residue on your grill or stove and thoroughly incinerate any grease or food particles. And at the request of numerous harried campground hosts, please don't leave your trash piled in your fire ring. It's not going to magically hop into the dumpster.

Don't sleep where you cook. If you pitch your tent right in front of your cooking fire, guess what your tent will smell like? Follow safe camping and cooking guidelines. No matter how bad the weather, never cook in your tent.

Hide your cooler. Human-food savvy bears love coolers; just pop off the top and dig in. Before you turn in, lock your cooler in your trunk or cover it with a dark blanket and lock it in your car. Remember to read up on local regulations—in places like Yosemite National Park, you'll be ticketed if you leave anything that looks or smells like food in your vehicle overnight; use the park's lockers. Don't leave empty cans or bottles in your tent or out in the open; they still smell like whatever was in them.

Clean up your car. Reducing clutter in your car lessens the chance a bear will look in the window and think there's something in there worth ripping off the door to get. It will also give you a chance to find any food, wrappers or packages that have disappeared under a seat or gotten stuck to the carpeting. If you have a child's car seat, this is a good time to get out the disinfectant and give it a good wipe down.

Don't roam around in the dark. Use a flashlight at night and make some noise if nature calls or you're coming back to camp after dark; there's much less of a chance you'll startle a bear if it can clearly see you coming.

Jack Hopkins, National Park Service

Asking for Trouble

Leaving food or other attractants visible or smell-able in your car overnight is asking for trouble. In some areas you can be ticketed and fined for leaving anything that looks or smells like food in your vehicle overnight. In other places you're permitted to store food locked in your trunk and out of sight. So be sure to check local regulations. And don't leave out things some bears have learned to recognize, like coolers and picnic baskets. Locked outfitter boxes or truck storage boxes can be a great and roomy alternative for in-vehicle storage.

Hard Facts About Hard-Sided Campers

It's possible for a determined bear to break into a camper or trailer. Resist the urge to leave the windows open when you leave for the day. Pull shades or curtains and store food, coolers, grocery bags, picnic baskets, and pet food out of sight. Don't leave trash bags outside.

While not an everyday occurrence, camper panels are no match for a bear that's learned the big rolling tin cans are full of goodies. *© Jim Tiffin (left), Curt Livingston (right)*

The number one source of food odors wafting out of hard-sided campers is the stove's exhaust system that vents outside. The filters, fan and exhaust ducts collect grease, moisture, dust and odors. The whole area should be regularly cleaned with a heavy-duty, ammonia-based cleaner.

"I have seen many unoccupied, empty, locked up trailers broken into by bears at the exhaust duct. This area is a real odor magnet, and a place that's easily forgotten when it's clean up time," says retired bear biologist Tom Beck, who's an avid camper.

Selecting a Camp Site

If you arrive at your campsite before dark, you can pick out a good spot to hang your packs if there aren't bear boxes or other systems available, and you don't have a bear-resistant canister.

No matter how tired you are, if your chosen site shows signs of a recent bear visit you should leave, even if it means camping somewhere you're not supposed to be. When you get back to the trailhead, report the site to a ranger or someone in authority.

Try to avoid pitching your tent near berry patches, streams, trails or dense cover. The farther out in the open you are, the less likely it is that a black bear will come into your camp.

Trees for hanging food and packs should be at least 100 yards downwind of your camp. If there are no trees, and you don't have a bear canister, double or triple bag everything in freezer bags or turkey-roasting bags, put in a dark stuff sack, and leave on the ground at least 100 yards downwind of your camp. When you go home, buy a bear canister for next time.

Your cooking area should also be at least 100 yards downwind. Your sleeping area, cooking area, and hanging trees should form a triangle. Remember, winds can change; be prepared to relocate if they do.

A bear-smart campsite. *Courtesy of Chuck Bartlebaugh, Be Bear Aware*

Going Tentless

Experts strongly recommend you don't sleep out under the stars in bear country. In many areas, it's illegal, and if found you'll get a ticket.

There are numerous instances of both black and grizzly bears investigating a sleeping bag, and licking, nipping or biting the big object in the cocoon. It would be simple for a bear to mistake a large object on the ground for carrion—an easy, protein- and fat-packed meal. Enjoy your dinner under the Big Dipper (away from your tent), but don't take a chance you could become dinner for something else. Sleep inside.

Steve Herrero says, "Sleeping under the stars is one of my favorite things to do while camping, but I choose areas in which to do this carefully. My data strongly suggests that people sleeping without tents were more likely to be injured, even killed, than were people who slept in tents."

What's a good place? Herrero says to choose an open area, well away from trees, big rocks, bushes and other landscape features that would make good cover for a bear. Above treeline is okay, as long as you're not in grizzly country. If you're in grizzly country, there is no good place to sleep under the stars.

Pack Hanging System

Bears in the Smokies have not figured out how to defeat this clever pack hanging system that originated in Banff National Park in Canada. Trees in the park were too tall to allow food bags to be hung conventionally. Metal poles didn't work; people couldn't balance their packs on top of the poles, but bears could easily balance themselves. The system as shown can keep up to four packs suspended out of a bear's reach between two trees. It's very important that the first pulley be out of reach, or bears learn how to reel in dinner.

© Warren Bielenberg

Backpacking Where Bears Roam

Many areas with heavy bear activity require backpackers to use bear-resistant canisters, and often provide them free or for a nominal fee. They can also be bought or sometimes rented at outdoor stores. The canisters are cylindrical, so bears can't get their paws on a seam, lid or latch. Some experts recommend you hang your bear canister if you can; if you can't, they can be left on the ground in the open, well away from your tent. Think nutrition and weight when you're packing. Freeze dried foods are light, easy to pack, and relatively odor free. Leave the aged salami at home.

The newest bear-resistant canisters are lighter, roomier, and easier to pack. *www.BackpackersCache.com*

Pack toiletries in plastic bags as well. You'll have less trash to worry about, and you can use the empties to secure things you need to pack out. Don't leave your packs where the wind could blow smoke and yummy cooking smells their way; even today's ballistic fabrics absorb smoke and odors, and you don't want your pack to smell like dinner.

Trash and bits of food should be packed in plastic bags and stored with your food. Some people who don't like the idea of their food rubbing elbows with their trash bring a separate stuff sack for garbage. If you must burn trash or bits of food, burn well away and downwind from your sleeping quarters and make sure everything is completely incinerated.

When you're done for the day, pack up all your food, toiletries, trash, the clothes you cooked in, pots, pans, and anything else that might remotely have an odor, and hang your pack at least 10 feet off the ground, and 4 feet out from the trunk of the tree.

Backpacking and Backcountry Camping Essentials:

- Bear spray; ideally at least one canister and holster per person
- Safety whistle
- Unscented toiletries
- Low odor foods
- Freezer bags or turkey-roasting bags for storing food and garbage
- Bear-resistant food canisters or rope/cord for hanging packs

When you're carrying literally everything you need to survive in your pack, you don't want to lose it to a hungry bear. And you don't want to take a chance of getting hurt defending it, either.

Do Menstrual Odors Attract Bears?

The short answer is "No," followed by "But," because there's no statistical or even anecdotal evidence that black bears or grizzly bears are attracted to menstruating women. Steve Herrero analyzed the circumstances of hundreds of grizzly bear attacks on humans and concluded there was no evidence linking menstruation to any of the attacks. A study by Lynn Rogers recorded responses of black bears to both menstruating women and used tampons, and found that menstrual odors were essentially ignored by black bears of all ages.

In an extensive review of black bear attacks across North America, no evidence of attraction was found. BUT any strong or unusual odors can attract bears, and many feminine products are highly scented. Kerry Gunther, bear management biologist at Yellowstone National Park, did an extensive review of existing data, and recommends that women use internal tampons rather than external pads and use unscented cleaning towelettes. Used tampons should be double-bagged and stored as you would store food, never buried (bears may dig them up). Tampons can be burned in a campfire, but the fire must be super-hot to completely incinerate them. Remove any remnants and store them with the garbage.

Electric Fencing Makes for Happy Campers

The terrain at breathtaking Lake Louise in Banff National Park in the Canadian Rockies naturally causes bears to travel along the boundaries of a popular 220-site tenting campground as they do their best to utilize the valley bottom and bypass the community.

After a long history of human-bear conflicts and long periods of closure for the tenting section, in 2001 and 2002 camping was restricted to hard-sided vehicles only. But in an effort to reopen the campground to tenting and still keep people and bears apart, Parks Canada experimented with electric fencing 10 test sites.

Park staff was worried that people would feel they were in camping prison, but the security and effectiveness of the electric fence proved very appealing. In 2003 the entire tenting section was electric-fenced.

The fence safely guides bears around the tenting area as they travel through the valley and makes the terrain more predictable for bears, enhancing both bear and public safety. It prevents bears from being attracted into the campground to search for food. Closures are a thing of the past.

Campground staff patrols the fence each day to ensure it's working properly. Wildlife specialists respond to any intrusion alarms and troubleshoot any problems while the fence is energized. During the winter when the tenting site is closed, the electric fence is turned off and all gates are opened to allow unrestricted wildlife and human movement through the area.

Parks Canada says it's proven to be a low-cost, low-maintenance alternative to closures and allows bears and people to continue sharing the landscape.

Catch Fish, Not Bears

The best fishing spots are often in great bear habitat. Bears like to feed on vegetation along streams and the shores of lakes and ponds. Bears like to catch and eat fish. Some bears even learn to clean up after fishermen. Or wait for you to do the fishing for them before showing up for dinner. Unless you are fishing from a boat out in the middle of a big lake, fishing in bear country is a good way to encounter bears.

If you're camping around a lake or stream you need to be extra-careful not to attract bears. Take time to look for tracks and scats, heavily worn trails, birds scavenging along the banks or shore, or fish remnants (heads, tails, intestines). If you find a whole fish lying on the bank, leave the area; it probably belongs to a bear that will be back shortly.

A fast-flowing stream makes it tough to hear an approaching bear, and for the bear to hear you. Most people fish quietly, and concentrate on watching their line, not their surroundings. Take a bear break now and then and look around.

If you have a good day and catch some fish, clean them right away on the spot; don't take them back to camp. Steve Herrero suggests piercing the air bladder and tossing the fish guts into deep water in a stream or lake so they won't wash up on shore, unless regulations prohibit it. If that's the case, opt for burning them in a very hot fire. Just be sure to clean your fish far away from where people live or are camped; use a fish cleaning shed if one is available. Double bag your fish in zipper-style freezer bags.

© Anan Interpretive Staff, US Forest Service, NatureWatch Program

Bear expert Gary Brown strongly recommends you don't keep or cook fish in a backcountry camp. But if you're fishing for your dinner, then be sure to wrap and pack out all the remains, just like any other garbage.

And after you eat, pack up the clothes you were wearing and store them in a plastic bag, with your food and other attractants. Whatever you do, don't leave them in your tent or sleep in them. Wash up with a strong unscented soap before you turn in.

If you're fishing for salmon or other fish that travel up rivers in the summer and fall, you're probably going to be sharing the bank with bears trying to take advantage of this high-calorie food source.

The splashing of a hooked fish may attract a bear. Let out slack or cut your line to keep the bear from snagging your catch and learning fishermen equal bear food. But if a bear does manage to hook your fish, don't try to defend your catch.

If you're hiking in to fish, read the section on hiking before you hit the trail, keep an eye peeled for signs of bears in the area, and make some noise—especially when you're moving through dense vegetation or coming around blind curves.

If you're going fishing in grizzly country, do your homework. Responses that work with black bears often backfire with grizzlies, and vice versa. See Chapter 4 for a quick look at grizzly behavior.

Goodbye Bear #583

Adapted with permission from an article written in 1992 for the National Park Service website. Author Malinee Crapsey is still hard at work as an interpretive specialist in Sequoia and Kings Canyon National Parks. And this story is still the story of far too many bears in far too many places.

He probably started his short life close to where it ended, one of two 10-ounce cubs born in the rotted base of a large fir tree. The next year and half were spent with his mother learning to forage for what nature provides: winter-killed carrion, spring's meadow grasses, the yellow jackets and ants of summer, acorns and berries in the fall.

By his second spring, his mother drove him away; it was time for her to get on with the business of producing more cubs, and for him to go out on his own and grow up in the solitude normal to adult bears.

That spring he discovered human food. His first reward might have been an apple core left along a trail or lunch leftovers abandoned at a picnic table. Perhaps it was a bag of trash left sitting outside a bear-proof garbage can. No matter; he quickly learned that where there are humans, there is always easy food.

After a string of reports and at least one aggressive act he was trapped by wildlife biologist Dianne Ingram. She weighed him, put a colorful tag in his ear for easy identification, and gave him his name, #583. Because he was now a "problem bear," he also got a radio collar so biologists could follow his movements.

Park staff spent many hours radio-tracking #583, chasing the young bear away from trouble, throwing rocks and yelling. They talked to people about why it was important to keep food away from bears.

In July, #583 entered a building in search of food and knocked down a man while he was trying to escape. Later he bluff-charged a woman and child and entered an occupied restaurant kitchen and helped himself to lunch. Despite the staff's best efforts his rap sheet grew longer and longer.

Bears in the park are not destroyed just for finding garbage or stealing food, but because even a small bear can do tremendous harm to a person, aggressive or destructive behavior can seal their fate. Numerous relocations of food-conditioned bears within these parks have failed; the bears either returned to their territories or died. Zoos cannot take these wilderness misfits. So the order was signed to destroy #583.

His behavior was typical of food-conditioned bears, which often nap during the day waiting for people to go to sleep, then get up and take advantage of what's been left behind. The youngster's radio collar told the story: by 8:15 p.m. he was up and moving.

At 8:45 p.m. Dianne intercepted him, fired a dart filled with tranquilizer and trailed him for ten minutes until the drug took affect and he fell asleep. Everyone helped roll #583 onto a stretcher and carried him to the truck, trying not to stumble on the dark trail.

After a short drive to a secluded area, Dianne and another biologist took the bear from the truck, laid him gently on the ground, and shot him through the head. They knelt to take off his ear tag and collar and pushed his body over a steep embankment. His final resting place was the only natural thing about his death.

After a long, unhappy silence the "if only" discussion began: "If only he hadn't gotten that first taste. If only we could reach people all the time to tell them about food and bears."

When bears have to die, bear biologists feel like failures. But it is the people who couldn't be bothered opening the bear-resistant garbage can, cleaning up after their picnic, or taking their trash back to the car who failed #583.

You can help write a happier ending to the next bear story, and be part of a whole new chapter in the saga of human-bear coexistence. ❖

© Isaac Chellman

The Journey Back to Wild

Smart enough to learn that if you jump on the roof of a Volkswagen "Bug" the resulting drop in air pressure causes the doors to pop open. Determined enough to scale part of El Capitan to bag a climber's provisions. Clever enough to outwit, outlast, and outplay your average tourist. The bears of Yosemite National Park are truly the Einsteins of the bear world. Over the years they earned a reputation for being super-smart, super-resourceful, and super-hard to deter from habits learned over decades and passed down from generation to generation.

Between 1989 and 2002 there were over 9,300 bear incidents reported at Yosemite National Park, and well over a million dollars in property damage. In 1998, the high-water mark for human-bear

Delaware North at Yosemite

incidents, bears broke into thousands of vehicles and did more than $630,000 in property damage. Several bears that proved too aggressive to remain in the population were killed, including a mom and three cubs.

That was the year biologist Steve Thompson had enough of politely shielding visitors from the lethal effects of their carelessness. He invited the *Washington Post* to cover the death of the bear family. The resulting article caused quite a media uproar, and helped create public pressure to find a better solution.

Congressman Henry Waxman's chief of staff Phillip Schiliro brought his wife on vacation to Yosemite, stopped in to chat with rangers, and ended up spending the night seeing the problem first-hand. One thing eventually led to another, Congressman Waxman worked with the appropriations committee, and Yosemite finally got the money they needed to start fixing what Steve Herrero called "a problem in a class by itself."

Adding to the serendipity that summer was the creation of a widely seen and extremely well-done documentary, initiated by Congressman Waxman's wife Jody, a documentary filmmaker with the credentials to get a crew from National Geographic.

A comprehensive study in 2000 traced three out of four incidents directly to human error, usually improperly stored food or garbage. With newly acquired funds and being highly motivated to fix the problem,

© Heather Fener, Wildlife Conservation Society

Yosemite got to work finalizing the bear-proofing of the frontcountry campgrounds, installing food storage lockers at trailheads so hikers didn't have to leave food in their cars, mandating the use of bear canisters in the backcountry, testing methods of educating and motivating visitors, and issuing hundreds of food-storage violation notices. (Tickets and fines always seem to be motivating. A lot of people prefer carrots, but some only respond to sticks.)

Some of these tactics may sound simple, but developing the necessary tools and implementing their use put human resilience, resourcefulness and ingenuity to the test. By 2006 bear incidents in Yosemite National Park had dropped an average of 70 percent. In 2015, despite being in the fourth year of a drought, bear incidents overall were down 95 percent and frontcountry incidents were at the lowest level ever recorded.

The story of how Yosemite went from one of the most destructive and chronic situations in North America to one of the most bear-proof today is a testament to the determination and adaptability of hundreds of unsung heroes, from park employees and researchers to visitors who wanted to make a difference. It took trial and error, experimentation, and some old-fashioned good luck to do what many observers thought was impossible: fundamentally change how bears and people coexist in one of America's most popular and beloved national parks. It's an enlightening and intriguing story told with unrelenting honesty and in great detail by wildlife ecologist and human-wildlife conflict expert Rachel Mazur in her fascinating book, *Speaking of Bears: A Tale of Rewilding from Yosemite, Sequoia and Other National Parks.*

The Yosemite Valley has been a hot spot for human-bear conflicts ever since the first European settlers arrived in 1855. Those early pioneers quickly exterminated the grizzly bear, but black bears were seen as less threatening and allowed to remain. In 1864 fear that the valley was being overdeveloped led to Yosemite and the Mariposa Grove of Big Trees becoming the first natural protected areas in the United States.

Yosemite National Park occupies an area about the size of the state of Rhode Island in central California's rugged Sierra Nevada mountain range. The broad Yosemite Valley, the most heavily visited area of the park, remains a veritable Eden for bears, with nutritious natural foods available during every month of bear activity. As well as a magnet for humans anxious to explore and enjoy.

Back in the days of rudimentary roads and no way to haul trash, pit dumps were the popular and practical way to dispose of garbage and food waste. By the 1930s as many as 60 bears roamed throughout the valley, enjoying an abundance of both natural and unnatural foods. As happened in many other places, human misunderstanding of bears led to a series of decisions that created more problems than they solved.

In an attempt to draw bears away from the developing east end of the valley, artificial feeding areas were established in 1937 in the valley's western portion, as well as in other less-developed areas of the park. The feeding sites quickly became major tourist attractions, as people came to watch the bears chow down as much as 60 tons of human food scraps every year. Park concessionaires capitalized on the public's fascination with the bears, and ran nightly caravans out to feeding areas that were outfitted with spotlights and bleachers.

By the 1940s biologists and park managers began to suspect that artificial feeding was changing the very nature of Yosemite's bears, but

The original hope that allowing bears to feed at garbage dumps would eliminate conflicts elsewhere proved to be sadly mistaken. *Yosemite, 1942; National Park Service*

changing human nature took another couple of decades. When the last dump was closed in 1971, the nightly bear show came to an end.

But the bears weren't willing to give up their traditional food sources so easily. Bears used to fattening up on human food turned to raiding campsites and breaking into vehicles in search of the food they'd come to depend on. In the interests of protecting both bears and people, in 1975 Yosemite implemented what is today one of the oldest and most comprehensive bear management programs in the national park system.

Wildlife managers have successfully tracked the movements of black bears in developed areas in Yosemite for over a decade using radio telemetry. However, once a bear leaves a developed area, its movements are difficult to track. Yosemite Conservancy contributed nearly $70,000 to purchase GPS collars to track the bears beyond the Valley and provide currently unknown information about how bears use the majority of the park's wild habitat. It's hoped that both types of tracking will allow park personnel to prevent incidents and help stem bears' reliance on human food sources.

There is no limit to the amount of useful research wildlife managers would love to do, but they are limited by their budgets. That's why support groups like Yosemite Conservancy are invaluable. Since 1989, Yosemite Conservancy donors have contributed $2.1 million to support bear protection and education programs, including the construction and installation of over 2,000 bear-proof food storage lockers throughout the park. The organization also rents bear-proof food canisters for backpackers and supports educational programs.

"We're committed to helping the park protect Yosemite's wildlife so future generations can experience thrills like seeing a black bear ambling through a valley meadow," said former Yosemite Conservancy President Mike Tollefson. "Those are memories that last a lifetime and encourage people to be stewards of the park." ❖

Today Yosemite's bears are making the journey back to truly wild.
© Caitlin Lee-Roney, Yosemite National Park Wildlife Biologist

---

From the Yosemite National Park Employee Suggestion Box: Save the Bears! Dart and tranquilize offending humans, and relocate outside the park.

On the Road in Bear Country

Florida Fish & Wildlife Conservation Commission

Driving Bear Aware

You're driving near dusk on a roadway that goes through some natural area. You glance away for a few seconds and something big and bulky darts in front of you. You slam on the brakes but it's too late – you hear a sickening thud and feel your car shudder as you try to get it under control. When you can finally stop and survey the damage, you see the front of your car is twisted and crumpled, as is the bear you just ran over. Her cubs are whimpering wide-eyed next to her body.

© Rich Beausoleil

A bear killed by a car. *US Forest Service*

All over the U.S. and Canada, vehicles and bears are colliding more often, with predictable results. Bears die. Vehicles are severely damaged. People are injured. And if you don't carry comprehensive insurance coverage, you can be stuck with a big bill. Insurer State Farm estimates that collisions with wildlife cost billions of dollars and kill millions of animals each year.

The Federal Highway Administration believes the frequency of large animal-vehicle collisions is probably much greater than statistics show for several reasons, including the fact that damages below $1,000 are typically not submitted to insurance companies.

There are more than four million miles of roads in the U.S. and three-quarters of a million miles in Canada, including the Trans-Canada highway which bisects important wildlife watersheds like Banff National Park. Roads are generally good for people and bad for wildlife. They fragment habitat, making it hard for wide-roaming species to access enough territory to thrive. Multi-lane highways create barriers that can be impossible to cross.

The first wildlife crossing in the U.S. was a black bear underpass built in Florida in 1955. Twenty years later the first overpass was constructed over Utah's I-15. Canada's mountain parks started erecting barriers to keep wildlife off the roads in 1981. Today there are hundreds of wildlife crossings of various types in use in much of the U.S. and Canada.

By far the greatest number of animal fatalities involve ungulates—deer, elk and moose. But bears die on the roads with alarming frequency. Florida's black bear management program coordinator Dave Telesco says the state is the roadkill capital of North America, with an average of 200 bears hit and killed each year—that's 4.8 percent of the state's bear population. They've already installed 91 underpasses to give wildlife, including bears and the endangered Florida panther, a better chance of surviving the daily game of dodge-em, and they plan to install 11 more plus an overpass for I-4 in central Florida. Hidden cameras show that once bears discover underpasses provide safe passage, they head right for them.

The six wildlife overpasses and 38 underpasses along the Trans-Canada Highway in Banff have reduced the number of wildlife-vehicle collisions by more than 80 percent for most animals and 96 percent for elk and deer. They've been monitored with track plates, cameras, and wires that snag for hair samples for genetic analysis. There's no doubt that these crossings and regularly maintained fences facilitate wildlife movement. Cameras have captured

In any language, the message is the same: slow down and be on the lookout for furry jaywalkers.
© Danielle Sell, Banff National Park

Underpasses provide safe passage for animals.
© Susan Hagood, The Humane Society of the United States

Grizzly bear triplets make a run for it in Yellowstone National Park. *© Deby Dixon*

the safe passage of thousands of animals, including elk, mule deer, moose, grizzly bears, black bears and mountain lions.

While wildlife use both the underpasses and overpasses, researchers discovered that grizzly bears, wolves, elk, moose and deer prefer high, wide and short overpasses, while black bears and cougars choose the cover provided by long, narrow underpasses.

An even more interesting side effect of safe passage came to light in a study published in 2014 in the *Journal Proceedings of the Royal Society B* by Michael Sawaya and colleagues. At first grizzly bears were reluctant to use the crossings; it took five years for the bears to gradually start using them. Because of that and the high cost, some people questioned whether the crossings were worth it and whether more such structures should be built in other parks.

So Sawaya and his colleagues used strands of barbed wire to collect thousands of bear hair samples both in and around 20 crossings in Bow Valley and the surrounding area between 2006 and 2008. Their DNA tests revealed a large number of black and grizzly bears were using the crossings. While previous research suggested that most of the bears using the crossings were too young to breed, the new study found that almost half of black bears and nearly 30 percent of grizzly bears that used the crossings bred successfully during the study.

While previous studies had shown that highway barriers were causing inbreeding, the new study suggests that the wildlife crossings are starting to restore the gene flow between grizzly bears on both sides of the highway, as bears can now roam much farther seeking mates. Besides using the wildlife crossings to look for mates, there is evidence that animals also use them to find food, shelter, or escape from predators.

Black bears on black roads are hard to see. Drive carefully, obey the speed limits, and keep your eyes peeled. Statistics show that most collisions occur at dawn, dusk and at night, or under conditions that make animals hard to see and at speeds that make it hard to stop.

If you do hit a bear, please report it; statistics provide ammunition for making roadways safer for bears and people. If you injure a bear, call 911 and wait for wildlife authorities to arrive. Don't try to help; the bear is most likely in pain and frightened, and you could get injured. ❖

Insurance Doesn't Always Cover It

Many insurance policies don't cover wildlife damage, including damage caused to vehicles by wildlife collisions on the highway. Taking steps to bear-proof your home and driving sensibly when wildlife might be on the road (one clue is an abundance of wildlife crossing signs) is much cheaper than replacing your car or your kitchen.

US Forest Service

19

Viewing and Photographing Bears

When I was working on the first edition of *Living With Bears*, the irascible and irrepressible Chuck Bartlebaugh, who's been advocating for bears since 1976, suggested I write a very short book with a singular message: "Leave Bears Alone." Most bear experts agree that if people and bears never shared space, there would be no human-bear conflicts.

But to observe a bear being a bear in the wild is an eye-opening and sometimes life-changing experience. It's an opportunity many seek and few realize. In parks and other public lands people are admonished not to approach bears. But visitors routinely cite seeing

© Anan Interpretive Staff, US Forest Service, NatureWatch Program

a bear as one of the highlights of their trip. That drive to check off something on their bucket list can push some people to cross the line and get too close or offer food in hopes of going home with that experience they came looking for.

The challenge of finding safe, smart ways to allow people a real or virtual glimpse into the lives of one of North America's most charismatic animals is one worth chewing on for every entity that manages bear populations.

Interagency Grizzly Bear Committee Bear Viewing Guidelines

DON'T APPROACH BEARS...EVER! The safest bear viewing is in areas where viewing is an established and managed practice. See the appendix for a list of managed bear viewing areas. Sometimes your vehicle provides a ring-side seat without bothering the bears.

Observe, Don't Disturb. The guidelines say, "If you scare a bear, you have failed as a bear watcher." The general recommended safe viewing distance is 100 yards away, or the length of a football field. There are no jumbotron video monitors in the woods, so bring really good binoculars. If your presence causes an animal's behavior to change in the slightest way, you're too close.

Habituated Bears. Many bears that have adjusted to being watched are at least partially habituated. That means they've had to learn to tolerate people to some extent simply to travel, forage, raise their young, sleep and eat. Bears that have become habituated in safe, no-hunting zones like parks may come quite close to you, and may not seem to actually notice you are there. These bears may be relatively safe to watch quietly from your car, but never approach, make loud noises, or do anything threatening. Tolerance only goes so far. **There are no tame bears in the wild, in zoos, in captivity, or anywhere else.**

As our guide drolly warned us in Alaska, don't bring along a tuna sandwich when you're going bear viewing. In fact, it's good to avoid loud colors and heavily scented products. Bring good binoculars, and leave your food at home. For the full guidelines, see *www.igbconline.org* under Bear Safety.

Million-Dollar Bears

What's a bear worth? About $10 million a year to Yellowstone's regional economy, according to a 2014 study coauthored by Yellowstone National Park's bear biologist Kerry Gunther. Yellowstone's bears also create 155 jobs in the region.

Research shows that Old Faithful isn't the number one reason people come to Yellowstone. It's the wildlife viewing. Especially bears. In fact, the study accidentally uncovered the surprising fact that seeing a bear is so important that visitors said they would be willing to pay another $41 on top of the $25-per-vehicle entrance fee to ensure they'd have a good chance of seeing a bear.

Providing the public with the easy opportunity to watch bears comes at a price. Yellowstone park rangers and other employees spent 2,542 hours managing more than 1,031 bear jams in 2011.

Authors Leslie Richardson, Tatjana Rosen, Kerry Gunther and Chuck Schwartz tackled the study because parks and most other entities are dealing with budget crunches that have management asking tough questions about where funds are best spent. One of those questions was whether Yellowstone could save money if they stopped paying rangers to babysit people at bear jams.

Deby Dixon took this photo of Scarface, one of the most famous grizzlies in Yellowstone, from the safety of her car as he wandered along the Lamar River.

In the 1980s Yellowstone tried to eliminate roadside bears by hazing, harassing, and moving them to the backcountry with little success. The super-intelligent bears quickly learned to recognize individual employees and their vehicles, and scooted off when they spotted them—only to return as soon as the coast was clear.

With the recovery of the grizzly bear population, the Yellowstone ecosystem may now be at carrying capacity for grizzly bears, which need lots of territory to roam. There's nowhere to move bears that isn't already occupied by other bears.

So in 2008 Gunther decided to try managing the people instead of the bears. The park staff started policing a few of the bear jams instead of trying to get people and bears to move away.

The public loved it, and the bears adapted well. The tactic allows the bears to take advantage of highly productive roadside habitat which provides a lot of natural foods, including ungulate carcasses, elk calves, whitebark pine nuts, clover, biscuit root, pocket gophers, Yampa roots, and rose hips. And people are allowed the rare opportunity to closely observe bears being bears.

But 1,000 bear jams a year is too many for rangers and volunteers to supervise. Staffing up would cost a lot more money. Leaving the bears and the people to sort it out on their own could cause problems. There's always a chance that sooner or later some visitor will break the rules and feed the bears, or approach too closely for a photograph and get hurt.

Yellowstone gets an estimated $4 million for park projects from their share of the entrance fees. If visitors paid another $50 for bear viewing, it would put an additional $8 million into park coffers that could logically go towards bear programs. Talk about bears working for a living.

Providing safe opportunities for people to observe bears could allow people to connect with wildlife while at the same time funding important programs to ensure that wildlife will be around to observe for generations to come.

Photographing Bears

Photographing bears requires skill, patience and old-fashioned good luck. Pros can spend many hours waiting for that perfect shot, and still go home without it. That's why people end up doing dumb things, like dangling donuts and hiding out in the bushes. Today's digital cameras and super-smart phones make seizing the moment easier than it used to be.

Your car makes a great photo blind, allowing you to remain invisible and non-threatening. Talk to the rangers or locals about good places to observe wildlife. Animals are often easier to photograph in protected areas where they know they are safe. (Yep, they know.) That doesn't mean they are tame. There are no tame wild animals.

Lighting will be better and animals easier to spot if you go early in the morning, late afternoon, or early evening.

You can roll down the window, but don't get out of your car to get closer. There's no way to predict when you'll cross the line and invade the individual bear's comfort zone. Some bears seem comfortable allowing people to get within a few dozen yards. Others bristle when you're a football field away. And a bear's reaction on any given

Bear paparazzi on Sparks Lane in Great Smoky Mountains National Park.
© Warren Beilenberg

day depends on what it was doing when you interrupted it. Getting too close can make the bear defensive. That's how a bear that was just minding its own business becomes an aggressive-bear-encounter statistic.

A safe distance is one where your presence doesn't change the bear's behavior in any way. "Most people don't know how to read the signals bears give. Even a slight yawn is a sign of stress and means the photographer should step back," says veteran photographer Bill Lea.

Never deliberately sneak up on or surprise a bear. Many bear attacks are caused by a sudden encounter that triggered a bear's defensive instincts.

Don't tempt bears with food. Just one handout teaches a bear to associate people with a food reward. People are often nipped and scratched by bears they are trying to feed. Bears that nip people usually lead short lives.

Avoid newborn and young animals, including bear cubs. Mom is around, and she's not happy you're there.

Work in pairs in the backcountry. One person can keep an eye on the lens, and the other can keep an eye on the big picture. There are way too many photos of a blur of fur and teeth—the last photo that photographer ever took.

How Do the Pros Get Such Great Shots?

Some pros spend a lifetime learning how to safely observe and photograph in the wild. Others pros rely on special access permits to controlled wildlife management areas and zoos, game farms or wildlife sanctuaries. Close-ups of snarling bears often star a captive bear that earns its living performing. The teeth-baring snarls are the result of the bear trying to lick a big blob of sticky peanut butter off the roof of its mouth.

Pros use appropriate telephoto lenses—in the 600mm range—and other equipment that the average hobbyist wouldn't want to invest in or lug around. One good lens can cost more than $8,000 and weigh 13 pounds. When I want a great photo, I buy postcards. The lighting and composition is perfect, and they fit nicely in a photo album.

Safely viewing bears in the wild is an unforgettable experience that can produce memories and photos that will last a lifetime. ❖

You have to wonder who's watching who. Curious grizzly cubs in Yellowstone National Park. *© Deby Dixon*

Dedicated pros mingle with enthusiastic bear watchers at a respectful and safe distance in Yellowstone National Park. *© Kerry Gunther, National Park Service*

Capturing One Perfect Bear Photo

by professional photographer Bill Lea
www.BillLea.com

Photographing bears always requires a lot of time, the best equipment and a great deal of luck. I had wanted to capture a brown-colored black bear mother and her cub on film with just the right look on their faces for years. I had spent countless hours in the woods with nothing to show for my efforts.

Needless to say, when I came across this black bear with her little brown cub I was excited about the possibilities. Yet I knew it wouldn't be easy to capture that one perfect bear photo. Using a long telephoto lens so I could keep a safe distance between us meant I would have very little depth of field. I knew they would have to get into a position where they were in nearly the same plane of focus. It was also overcast, which is what I needed in order to avoid the contrasting light of bright sunlight and dark shadows in the woods.

These conditions, however, meant I would be using a slow shutter speed. So, I needed the bears very close to each other, holding nearly perfectly still, and situated in a setting with no distractions with just the perfect look that would reflect their personalities. I knew the likelihood of this happening was slim, but after hours of waiting and a lot of luck, the mother bear approached the cub from behind and stood still for just a split second while her cub looked up. I fired off two shots and one turned out just as I had hoped. I may spend another ten years in the woods photographing and never again have such an opportunity.

Crossing Paths with Bears

20

Bear Signs and Sounds

When I do presentations about living and playing in bear country, the questions I'm asked most often are about the one thing least likely to occur: bear attacks. The idea of being hurt or killed by a powerful predator is the stuff nightmares are made of.

Understanding bear behavior, learning how to prevent conflicts, and knowing how to respond if you see a bear will arm you with the best weapon you could have: a bear-smart brain.

Donde Está el Oso Negro?

If you've ever traveled in a country where you don't speak the language, you know that being able to recognize, understand, and use even a few hundred words can make the difference between feeling helpless and confident. The better you understand what bear signs, postures, vocalizations and behaviors mean, the better prepared and less nervous you'll be if you actually cross paths with a bear.

EVIDENCE OF BEAR ACTIVITY

If you're in bear country and know what to look for, it's not hard to find signs of bear activity. Some are simply evidence that bears are, or have been, in the area. Others are a form of bear-to-bear communication. Once you understand what they mean, it's much easier to figure out what you should do.

Bear Tracks

Bear tracks can look eerily like human footprints. © *Bryan Peterson*

Black bear tracks are very distinctive; it's hard to mistake them for anything else, except maybe a barefoot human footprint. All bears have five toes; although sometimes only four claw marks are visible in front paw tracks. The front foot is wider than it is long; the hind foot is narrower, with a rounded heel and a wedge in the instep. Bears can't retract their claws, but in some terrain claw marks won't show up.

The size of a bear track is determined not just by the size of the bear, but also by the type of terrain. Tracks will spread out and look larger in mud and melting snow, but they might be barely visible on harder surfaces. The front foot averages 4 to 5 inches long and 6 to 7 inches wide. The hind foot is narrower, averaging 7 inches long and 5 to 6 inches wide.

Bears are normally solitary; if you find multiple tracks it's most likely a mother with cubs or yearlings. In June and July when bears mate, it could be a male and female traveling together. Or you could simply be on a trail that bears use regularly. Bear tracks are common in areas with enough rainfall to keep the ground soft and along beaches and other places where it's easy for a bear to leave impressions; tracks are harder to find in much of the drier western part of the continent except during rainy or snowy weather. So a lack of tracks doesn't necessarily indicate an absence of bears.

Bear Scat

It's easy to recognize a bear's very sizable droppings, which are usually deposited in coiled segments. Along with sheer size, bits of plant fibers, seeds, hair, insect parts, and the occasional candy bar wrapper distinguish bear droppings from human deposits. Droppings are usually dark brown or black, but can be green if bears are eating lots of springtime grasses, and resemble big, sloppy cow pies when fruits and berries are in season.

Turn the scat over; if the grass underneath is still green, the scat is fresh and the bear could be nearby. If the underside is dry and the grass is yellow or brown, the scat is old and the bear may have moved on.

The more bears eat, the more they scat. During summer bears deposit scat piles a couple of times a day. During berry season, a single bear might scat 15 times in a relatively small area. So finding multiple piles of berry-filled scat isn't necessarily an indication of multiple bears.

The tidy pile of droppings is from the spring; the big sloppy "cow-pie" is from the fall.
© Bryan Peterson

Overturned Rocks and Logs

Bears flip over rocks and boulders looking for ants, beetles, grubs, and plant roots. If the underside of the rock is still damp, the bear could still be close by. Bears will rip apart fallen trees and logs looking for insects, and dig into ant hills and beehives in search of a fat- and protein-packed meal. In cattle country, bears turn over cow pies in search of bugs. Bears also use their claws to dig for starchy roots, uncover seed and nut caches buried by squirrels, and dig out ground squirrels, voles and mice.

Marks on Trees

© Cory Phillips

Bears often climb trees for safety, and can leave distinctive claw marks going up and sliding down. In the spring when better quality food sources are in short supply, bears may chew or peel the bark of young conifers to get to sapwood, leaving hanging strips of bark and long vertical grooves in the trunk. Long black or brown fur caught in the bark and sap, or tooth and claw marks signify a rub tree, a sort of giant back-scratching post bears use to relieve the itch of parasites and loosen thick, matted winter coats. Scientists think that bears also rub and mark trees to send messages to other bears; the height of the claw marks is a good indication of the size of the bear that left them, and could be a way for adult males to establish dominance and avoid confrontations.

Fish Heads and Entrails

If you find fish heads and entrails along a stream or lake shore, it could be leftovers from fishermen, but it's more likely a sign of bears feeding on fish in the area. Read the "Outdoors in Bear Country" section for more details on how to be bear-smart in the outdoors.

Brush-Covered Carcass

Circling scavenger birds are a good indication of a carcass in the area. A dead elk or deer is a bonanza of protein and calories. If you find a carcass with meat on it turn around and backtrack (if you go back the way you came, there's less chance you'll surprise a snoozing bear) until you can make a very wide detour. A carcass that's been cached under twigs or debris has been claimed by a mountain lion or bear, and whatever buried it may be close by. If you are in grizzly country, this is a potentially serious situation; backtrack immediately and be on the alert with your bear spray ready. Mountain lions cache carcasses more often than bears do, and may choose to protect them.

BEAR BODY LANGUAGE AND SOUNDS

Bears are very capable of injuring or killing each other, but fatal encounters are uncommon. To keep the peace and avoid getting physical, bears send each other clear signals, and show their stress in many ways, from subtle signs like yawning or changing a body position to huffing, moaning, and teeth popping. In most bear-to-bear encounters, the bears read each other's messages and slowly separate. But if one bear ignores the signals and crowds the other bear's space or threatens cubs or food, the encounter can quickly escalate into a very physical confrontation. Fighting for real is a last resort; there are no bear vets roaming the woods, and injured bears have a much harder time foraging and feeding themselves and their cubs.

Most bear-to-bear encounters are quite civilized, characterized by tolerance, restraint, and a "live and let live and go on our separate ways" attitude. Many scientists believe that bears generally respond to humans much as they would to encountering another bear. If that is indeed the case, bears must wonder why so many people just don't understand the message.

Bear Body Language

Sitting down, looking away, yawning, standing still. All elaborate displays of disinterest or low levels of stress. These behaviors show respect or indicate that the bear is deliberately ignoring you and would like you to do likewise.

Nose up, ears forward, standing on all four paws. The bear is using its highly sensitive nose to identify something it doesn't recognize.

Standing on hind legs. Despite what you see in the movies, this is not an aggressive posture. Bears stand on their hind legs to get a better look and smell of something unusual they've detected, from a passing hiker to a decomposing carcass. If the bear moves its head from side to side it's just trying to expose its super-sensitive nose to more scent molecules.

© Bill Lea

Head down, ears laid back, body low to the ground. Ears laid back, as with horses and dogs, signals that the bear is uneasy, nervous, or feels threatened, and might defend itself by striking out.

Ears lowered, but not back all the way, no eye contact, cowering with head lowered, trying to look smaller. This is submissive behavior; it's typical of the way a young bear might respond to the presence of an older, dominant bear.

Pawing or slapping the ground or an object. With black bears this is almost always blustery behavior meant to intimidate and avoid a physical encounter.

Bear Talk

Bears are generally quiet, but they do vocalize when the need arises.

Tongue clicks and grunts. Bears click and grunt in amicable situations with mates, other bears, and occasionally with people. Mother black bears use tooth-clicks and grunts to communicate with cubs. These are the most common bear sounds.

Blowing air and huffing. A huff sounds like air brakes being applied and released on a semi, but is just a loud exhalation of air that usually means the bear is nervous or fearful. Even tiny cubs huff.

Snapping jaws and popping lips. Jaw-popping and teeth-clacking are a more insistent warning to back off. These sounds can precede or follow a bluff charge. Think of it as people yelling.

Cub sounds. Cubs produce long, loud, hoarse wails when they are frightened or separated from mom. Cubs also bawl and scream in distress, whine much like human offspring, and make a deep humming sound when nursing or comfy and warm.

Moaning. Bears that have fled up a tree to escape a real or perceived danger often moan in fear. Moans, which sound like a human moan, are not a sign of aggression.

Deep-throated pulsing. When a black bear faces you with its ears back, making a deep-throated, pulsing sound, the bear is very distressed and could charge.

Growling. Black bears don't growl. Sometimes deep moans could be mistaken for a growl, but are actually an indication of extreme fear and distress, not aggression or dominance. ❖

Barking Bears

If you hear a lot of woofing and "barking" there's probably a bear close by that's trying to let you know you've gotten too close for comfort. Many years ago when I lived in the Midwest and knew nothing about bears, I got lost in a Colorado forest near sundown. While I was wandering around trying to find my way out, I heard persistent woofing; luckily for me, I never found the "dog" that was "barking" at me. Blind luck must have sent me out of the bear's way, and eventually I stumbled within earshot of a family that had just arrived for the weekend. I've learned a lot about both bears and hiking since then.

21

Encounters with Bears

With growing numbers of people living, working and playing in bear country, it's inevitable that from time to time the two species will cross paths. The vast majority of chance encounters end quickly and peacefully, with startled bear and startled person going their separate ways.

When someone says "bear encounter" they can mean anything from seeing a bear a hundred yards away browsing on berries to walking in on one helping itself to the contents of their refrigerator.

The International Association for Bear Research and Management (IBA) has been trying to eliminate confusion by standardizing the terms used to describe the many facets of human-bear relations. Here are their descriptions in layman's terms.

© Sara Tuttle

Sighting: You see the bear, but there is no evidence that the bear sees you.

Encounter: Person and bear are both aware of each

other. You'll know the bear is aware of you if its posture or behavior changes in some way. It might make a point of ignoring you, leave the area, stand up to get a better look at you, or approach.

Incident: An encounter during which the bear's behavior requires a human response that could range from standing your ground to deploying your bear spray. Learning how to read bear behavior and how to respond appropriately can keep an incident from escalating into a potentially dangerous situation. An incident can end peacefully or could result in an attack with injuries.

Attack: Bear attacks are a rare type of incident during which the bear intentionally injures someone. A bear attack can be defensive (the bear is responding to what it perceives as a threat) or much more rarely, offensive (the bear attacks without being provoked).

Bearanoia: The unfounded and irrational fear that every bear is out to get you, your kids, and your pets. Most bears want nothing more than to be left alone, and will do their very best to avoid you. Education and awareness are great cures for Bearanoia.

BEARS IN THE BACKYARD: TOO CLOSE TO HOME

Removing attractants and bear-proofing your home and property goes a long way towards preventing encounters with bears on your home turf. But when bears and people share space, you may still find a bear in your yard from time to time.

What harm is there in letting the bear snooze in your yard, go for a swim in your pool, or clean up some fallen apples (you missed Chapter 14, didn't you?)?

If it's not doing anything wrong, isn't it mean to chase the bear away? In the long run, it's a lot meaner to let it stay. Because allowing bears to get comfortable around people teaches them that people places are safe and people are harmless.

Bears are enterprising, curious and constantly explore their environments in hopes of finding food. The journey from cute bear munching on your apples way in the backyard to scary bear trying to push open your door can be a very short one.

So instead of grabbing your phone and filming a video for YouTube, here's how to be a real hero before you and your neighbors have a real problem.

Make sure your dogs are secured (barking is good; chasing is very, very bad) and your kids are in the house.

If you can do so safely, step outside onto the porch or deck. Or open a window or door. Now give a good shout or handclap. If the bear doesn't bolt, lock eyeballs and stare. In this situation direct eye contact is a simple, powerful way to let the bear know this is your territory and it's not welcome.

If the bear doesn't leave, it may have been already been rewarded elsewhere. Don't approach; just keep staring and start making more noise. Clap and yell, bang pots and pans, and use your whistle or air horn. You can toss small rocks or softballs in the direction of the bear but don't throw hard or try to hit the bear; bears have been seriously injured and killed by thrown objects.

If the bear is in range and conditions are favorable, bear spray is an option (see Chapter 23). A high-powered squirt gun filled with water and a little vinegar can work too.

Once the bear leaves, call your wildlife agency, report the incident, and alert your neighbors. Share information about what attracts bears and how (and why) to deter them.

Try to figure out what drew the bear into your yard. In addition to the big three (garbage, bird feeders and fruit trees), bears can be attracted to homes by many less obvious things, from insects nesting in the walls to freshly baked pies cooling on the porch or dog food in the back of the truck.

Taking action before something bad happens is your chance to teach a bear a lesson that could prevent a lot of problems for you, your neighbors and the bears.

Help! There's a Bear in My Home, Car or Garage

What should you do if you come home and discover a bear prowling through your kitchen cupboards?

Secure your dog, then make sure the bear has a clear escape route. Open all your doors and get out of the bear's way. Then start encouraging it to leave. Yell and throw things in the bear's direction—you want the bear to know your house is not its home.

If a bear comes in while you're home, try not to panic. Bears startle easily, and can wreak havoc careening around, trying to escape from the "danger" you present. Don't block the exit; bears trying to flee have injured people who got in their way. If the bear can escape without running you over, start yelling, clapping your hands, and throwing things.

Don't approach the bear, just yell from wherever you are. Conjure up whatever mental image allows you to holler convincingly. There should be no doubt in the bear's mind that you mean business. Avoid high-pitched screaming, shrieking, and crying that sounds like wounded prey.

Make note of the bear's size, color, and any characteristics that stand out and take a photo if you can. No matter what the circumstances, report bear break-ins to vehicles, buildings and homes to your local wildlife agency.

Ears forward combined with an open and silent approach or persistent following can indicate the rare aggressive or predatory black bear. *© Cory Phillips*

Seasonal Spikes in Bear Sightings and Interactions

Many people understand that the potential for bear conflicts goes up in late summer and early fall when bears are engaged in an around-the-clock eating contest with a grand prize of "Congratulations! You get to live through the winter." But often people are less aware of the seasonal spike that occurs in late spring and early summer, before many high-quality natural foods are available. Not only are all bears looking for something to eat, juvenile male bears are roaming around on their own for the first time looking for somewhere to live, and mature males are tramping throughout their considerable home ranges searching for as many mates as they can interest in a little roll in the grass. Moms with cubs are working very hard to find enough food for the whole family.

Instead of trying to remember when you need to be on high alert, just be bear-prepared from the first day of spring through Halloween, or whenever bears are up and about in your area.

MEETING A BEAR IN THE WOODS

Bears live in the woods, so seeing one now and then is to be expected. When you're in the great outdoors, you're visiting the bear's home turf. You are the invader, not the other way around. So be a good guest and avoid creating problems for the resident wildlife.

Bears use trails too; if you see signs of bears in the area, make noise periodically, avoid dense brush and natural foraging areas, and stay alert and aware of your surroundings, particularly at blind corners. See "Outdoors in Bear Country" section for much more on avoiding encounters.

Most human-bear encounters last for the split second it takes the bear to identify you and run off. Most encounters aren't aggressive and end peacefully and uneventfully. How you should respond depends on the situation and the behavior of the bear.

Encounters that last more than a split-second can be either defensive (by far the most common) or offensive. Most bear behavior that seems aggressive to us is actually defensive.

The closer you are when a bear becomes aware of you, the more likely it is to react rather than run away. A nervous, anxious, defensive bear that thinks you're a threat to its own safety or well-being, food source, or cubs can make lots of noise, huff and puff, clack its jaws, sway side to side, paw the ground, roar, or even charge you. To the average person, that can be pretty scary. To a bear biologist, those are clear signs of a stressed out and agitated bear trying to avoid a physical confrontation that could result in injury. (Apparently most bears think we are the ones who could potentially injure them.)

Bear Sightings

If you see a bear and it doesn't lift its head, change its posture, or respond to you in any way, it probably doesn't know you're there. Or you may be far enough away that it knows, but doesn't find your presence threatening.

If the bear is ignoring you, don't try to get its attention. If you're in a vehicle or at least 100 yards away, just relax and enjoy a rare opportunity to observe a bear going about the business of being a bear for a few moments, and then move on. Sighting a bear in its natural environment is nothing to be alarmed about.

It can be hard to resist trying to get a better look. But many a determined photographer or overly-eager bear enthusiast has crept too close for comfort and invaded a bear's personal space. In bear language that's a sign of aggression. You could unwittingly turn a great opportunity for quiet observation into a harrowing or even deadly incident that could end badly for both you and the bear. So respect. Appreciate. Admire. Just don't approach bears. See Chapter 19 for more on viewing bears.

How to Behave When You See a Bear

Here are some general guidelines. How you behave and respond depends to some degree on where you are and what both you and the bear are doing.

Stop, take a deep breath, stay calm and assess the situation. Don't startle the bear or try to get its attention.

If the bear doesn't react to you. You're having a sighting. Try to back away quietly without getting the bear's attention. Watch for any change in the bear's behavior.

If the bear's behavior changes. The bear most likely knows you are there. You're having an encounter. Talk calmly in a low respectful voice that identifies you as a human. Wave your arms slowly.

Back away. Back away slowly without making any sudden movements. Even if the bear seems to be ignoring you, never try to get closer; that could provoke a defensive response from the bear.

Be ready. If the bear approaches you, stand your ground and remain still. Get out your bear spray and be prepared to use it when the bear is within 40 to 50 feet.

Don't approach. The bear will view your approach as aggression, and may feel the need to defend itself.

Don't run. Running triggers a chase response in many animals, including bears. Remember, bears can sprint at speeds of up to 35 mph. You can't outrun a bear.

Don't climb a tree. All black bears and many grizzlies can climb trees faster than you can say "BEAR." Adult black bears can climb a 100-foot tree in less than 30 seconds. Mother black bears send their cubs up trees with the click of a tongue when they sense danger. You don't want to be stuck in a tree with a couple of bear cubs while mama bear waits patiently below for you all to come down. And when a dominant bear chases another bear up a tree in a battle of "who's the top bear, anyway?" the treed bear often gets yanked to the ground and pummeled a few times to teach it a lesson. Bears survive being pummeled by other bears much better than people do.

Don't play dead. Don't drop to the ground and play dead unless you are positive you are dealing with a bear defending cubs or a carcass. Grizzly bears commonly defend their cubs; black bears seldom do. See Chapter 22 for how, when and why to play dead.

If a Black Bear Approaches You

There are several reasons why a bear might approach you instead of run away. The bear could be curious and trying to figure out what exactly you are. The bear could see you as a threat and want to establish its dominance. The bear could be human food-conditioned and looking for a handout. In extremely rare cases the bear could be sizing you up as prey.

Ears laid back is a sign of a nervous bear that feels threatened and wants you to go away. *© Cory Phillips*

If a bear stands up and approaches on two legs, it's probably curious and trying to get a better look at you, or looking for an escape route. It might turn its head from side to side in order to pick up more scent molecules that will help it identify you as a person. Even though it's approaching you, the bear probably feels crowded, and is encouraging you to leave its space.

So oblige. Stay calm, talk to the bear in a firm, low voice and back away slowly, making sure the bear has a way to retreat. Try to stay uphill and keep the bear in sight. Once you can no longer see the bear, hike out, but don't run.

If the bear follows you after you retreat, as long as you are positive you're dealing with a black bear, try to chase it off—yell, clap your hands, throw rocks, bang any gear you have with you, blow your whistle or pocket air horn, or use your bear spray.

"A good loud hand clap can sound very much like a gunshot. It works well for me and has always resulted in the bear leaving," says Rich Beausoleil.

If a Black Bear Charges You

Bear language can be counter-intuitive; it's hard to accept that a big ball of muscle, fur and clacking teeth is running at you full-tilt because it's afraid of you and wants you to go away.

Sometimes a very stressed out black bear will paw and slap the ground, huff, puff, clack and snort, and lunge or run directly at you; this is often referred to as a bluff charge. The bear is treating you much as it would treat another bear it considered a possible threat. A black bear will almost always screech to a halt before making contact, then turn around and run back. If this happens, fight your urge to flee; a bear could bluff charge a half-dozen times before backing off.

Research shows this type of behavior rarely signals an imminent attack, and that responding appropriately (standing your ground or backing away slowly and talking to the bear) almost always causes the bear to retreat. After the bear retreats, you should too.

When Black Bears Aren't Bluffing

If a black bear does make physical contact with you, 99.9 percent of the time you should fight back. Black bears have been driven away by "weapons" that have included rocks, cameras, water bottles, hiking poles and fingernails. Don't run. Don't play dead unless you are positive the bear is defending cubs.

BEAR ENCOUNTERS WHEN CAMPING

Bears don't belong in camp. If a black bear comes into your camp, picnic ground or other developed area, do everything you can safely do to drive it away.

Sometimes campground bears can seem "tame." They may totally ignore you while nosing around looking for anything good to eat. Chances are these bears have already gotten food rewards from other campers and have learned that people are no big threat.

Don't offer food, stand around taking photos, approach, or

crowd the bear; if the bear gets nervous or feels threatened it could lash out and someone could get hurt.

Keep dogs leashed; don't let them chase the bear unless you're camping with a KBD or trained hunting dog. Send kids to their quarters so they don't inadvertently provoke the bear.

Round up your fellow campers. Make sure you don't surround the bear. Then start yelling, making lots of noise, banging pots and pans, and blowing whistles, air horns and car horns.

Try to note anything distinctive about the bear and take a photo if you can do so safely. After the bear leaves, report the incident to the campground host and local agency. Authorities may want to close a campground or trail or issue an alert if there are several reports of bear activity from the same area.

Try to figure out what attracted the bear to the campsite. Check trash containers, picnic tables and anywhere else food might be accessible. If your fellow campers won't clean up their act, report them to the campground host or area management. Looking the other way isn't being nice, it's putting people and bears at risk.

If you are tent camping alone or in the backcountry, sleep with your bear spray close by and keep something substantial and easy to grab at hand. See Chapter 17 for more on camping in bear country.

If you wake up and hear something snuffling outside your tent or nosing the fabric, start talking in a firm monotone so whatever it is realizes there's a person inside the big nylon mushroom. Human-food conditioned bears sometimes bite or claw the outside of a tent. Turn on your flashlight or lantern, and get your bear spray ready. If the bear starts ripping through your tent, prepare to defend yourself. Noted bear-attacks expert Steve Herrero avoids sleeping next to the tent wall.

If you're woken up by a bear already inside your tent, start yelling your head off and fight back with anything handy. This is a potentially dangerous situation. ❖

22

When Black Bears Attack

The vast majority of black bear "attacks" result in injuries so minor people don't even seek medical attention. Most of the scrapes, cuts and nips inflicted by black bears occur around developed campgrounds or other areas where bears have become human-food conditioned or when bears inadvertently injure people they're trying to get away from.

When some bears get too comfortable with people they adopt a "your food is my food, your place is my place" attitude. Bears can become so used to humans they'll linger by roadsides and picnic grounds in hopes of getting a handout. It's easy to be injured by a bear that grabs your hand instead of your dangling donut. The recent fad of taking selfies with wildlife or trying to take a photo of your kids with the bear can have fatal consequences for both people and bears.

People have been seriously injured by bears that seemed "tame." Wild bears are never tame. And based on a number of incidents where people keeping "pet" bears have been seriously injured or killed, "pet" bears are never tame, either. If you're offered a chance to have your photo taken with a "tame" bear, just say no.

When Black Bears Kill People

Dr. Stephen Herrero has long been regarded as the world's leading expert on bear attacks. According to his research study published in the *Journal of Wildlife Management* in 2011, in the 109 years between 1900 and late fall of 2009, 63 people in North America were killed by non-captive black bears. On average that's less than one person each year. Of course even one person is one person too many.

To put that in perspective, 54 people in the U.S. die each year from lightning strikes and 50 people succumb to bee stings. Between 2006 and the end of 2008 domestic dogs killed 88 people; doctors treated another 2.7 million for dog bites. That means more people were killed by domestic dogs in just three years than have been killed by black bears in all of recorded history.

Most people encounter dogs much more frequently than they encounter bears. But there are no documented cases of a bear researcher or biologist—arguably the people who spend the most time with black bears in the wild, often under circumstances that are trying for the bear—being severely injured or killed by a black bear.

Even though the number of people killed by black bears remains very low, it's been creeping up every decade over the past 60 years. In fact about 86 percent of all fatal attacks occurred between 1960 and 2010, when the study period ended. Forty-nine were in Canada and Alaska, about three and half times as many as in the lower 48 states. And while there are more black bears up north than in the rest of North America, the difference in bear density alone doesn't account for the numbers.

Herrero speculates that the most likely cause for the overall increase in fatalities is the fact that ever-increasing numbers of people are camping, hiking, living, and working in bear country.

The majority of fatal attacks to date have occurred in remote areas where bears are not accustomed to encountering people. In 38 percent of the cases Herrero studied, human food or edible garbage was probably responsible for the bear being in the location in the first place. There were no cases in which a black bear attacked a person in defense of a carcass or while trying to take a carcass away from a hunter. In one instance a hunter was killed by a bear he had wounded.

Herrero believes that 88 percent of the fatal attacks by black bears were offensive and predatory, which means evidence indicates the bear regarded the person as prey. In sharp contrast, the majority of serious and fatal grizzly bear attacks are defensive—the bear was defending its cubs or a carcass or was surprised at very close quarters.

Fatal attacks took place in both the frontcountry and backcountry, causing Herrero to conclude that some attacking bears had experience with humans and others did not. Most had no known history of associating with people.

What makes a black bear decide people are part of the food chain? Herrero says that no one knows for certain. We do know that adult male black bears are the perpetrators in most, but not all, fatal attacks. About 30 percent of the bears had health problems that could have been a factor, as food-stressed bears may be willing to take more risks.

And we know that the behavior of an individual bear is dictated not only by bear biology, but by that bear's unique personality and traits, as well as everything it's learned and experienced. Like people, bears are very much individuals; no two bears are exactly alike. Many bears are shy, retiring, and pretty mellow. Some are playful and curious. Others are bold and assertive. A rare few are the bear version of "bad apples."

What Are the Chances?

We all know that murderers, serial killers, and psychos live among us, yet few of us look at every stranger we meet as a threat. The very rare black bear that sees humans as something good to eat is a real anomaly. If bears considered us part of the food chain, hundreds of people would end up on the ursine menu each year.

The odds are more than a million to one the average person will encounter the extremely rare black bear that intends to harm them. But it will give you confidence if you know how to recognize and respond to predatory behavior.

How to Respond to Predatory Behavior

Statistically you have a better chance of encountering a predatory black bear in a very remote area, but in May 2000 a female black bear accompanied by her yearling attacked and killed an experienced female hiker who had photographed the pair at a trail junction in Great Smoky Mountains National Park. Evidence at the scene indicated she might have run from the bears before being killed. So no matter where you're going, it's smart to know what you're doing.

In an offensive predatory attack, the bear may eye you intently and approach openly on all fours with its ears forward, deliberately follow you or seem to be circling you, coming closer on each approach. It doesn't huff, clack its teeth, blow or moan, or exhibit any of the vocal or other signs of a nervous defensive bear that just wants you to leave. So don't cower, play dead or show any weakness. Go on the offensive and try to drive the bear away.

Let the bear know you know it's there, and you're not afraid of it. Act like you believe you can take the bear with one hand tied behind your back. Clap loudly, make noise, make yourself look as big as possible, yell with authority (don't scream or shriek), blow your whistle or air horn, and convince the bear you're not going down without a fight.

If you're wearing a backpack or daypack, leave it on, it could provide some protection. If you're carrying bear spray, use it when the bear is still 40 to 50 feet away, and leave the area as soon as the spray stops the bear. See the next chapter for all about bear spray.

Don't turn your back on the bear, don't climb a tree, and don't run. If the bear stops or backs off, do likewise, always keeping the bear in view. If you can get downwind so it's harder for the bear to track you, all the better; this is one case where you don't want the bear to know where you are. In a true predatory situation, the bear may seem to disappear for a while, only to reappear later. Be very alert until you reach safety, and keep your bear spray handy.

If you are attacked, fight back with everything you have. People have successfully fought off a black bear with everything from trekking poles to canteens and fingernails. Rocks, knives, heavy flashlights, tree branches...any weapon is better than no weapon when you're fighting for your life.

How and When to Play Dead

If you're attacked by a defensive bear, you need to convince it you are not a threat. For grizzly bears, a defensive attack is almost always the result of surprising the bear at close range or when it's feeding on a carcass or protecting cubs. It's very rare for a black bear to attack defensively, although there are a few instances on record of black bears attacking to defend cubs when the bear had no way to escape. If you see or hear cubs before you're attacked, assume the attack is defensive regardless of the bear species and respond accordingly.

Experts recommend waiting as long as possible and then falling straight to the ground, face down, with your legs spread slightly to give you some leverage. Lock your fingers behind your neck. Protect your face and vital organs. Try to dig in so the bear can't flip you over. If it does, roll back onto your stomach. Don't cry, scream or fight back.

Once the bear thinks you are no longer a danger, it should stop attacking and move off. Lie completely still and count to 500; often the bear is somewhere nearby, watching to make sure you've learned your lesson. If you get up too soon, it may decide you are a slow learner and attack again.

Know Your Bears

While your response to a defensive or offensive approach is the same regardless of the species of bear involved, grizzly bears are much more likely than black bears to attack in defense of cubs or a carcass, or because they've been surprised at very close quarters. Fighting back if you're attacked by a defensive grizzly bear is a losing proposition, because the bear is not going to stop until it's neutralized the "threat" and feels safe.

Fatal Black Bear Attacks in Brief

Here's a statistical look at the 63 fatal modern-day black bear attacks detailed and analyzed by Stephen Herrero *et al* in "Fatal Attacks by American Black Bear on People: 1900–2009," published in the *Journal of Wildlife Management* in 2011.

- 86% of fatal attacks have occurred since 1960
- 91% of attacks were on parties of one (69%) or two people (22%)
- 38% involved human food or edible garbage
- 88% of fatal black bear attacks were predatory
- 92% of predatory attacks involved male bears
- 70% of fatal attacks took place during daytime
- 61% occurred in the backcountry; 39% in the frontcountry*
- 3.5 times as many fatal attacks took place in Canada and Alaska compared to the rest of the U.S.
- 30% of bears had health problems that may have contributed
- **No one killed by a black bear had bear spray** ❖

Statistical abstract reviewed and approved by Stephen Herrero.

Between 2010 and November 2015 five people were killed by wild black bears, and one more by a captive bear. The last fatality I recorded before this book went to press was an elderly Montana woman killed in October 2015 by one of the black bears she'd been feeding; apparently it got into her home and then fatally injured her while attempting to escape.

** **Backcountry** is a loosely used term that refers to land that is isolated, undeveloped, remote and difficult to access; often refers to areas that are not accessible by ordinary motor vehicles. **Frontcountry** is composed of outdoor areas that are easily accessible by vehicle and mostly visited by day users; developed campgrounds are also included. Frontcountry locations tend to be more crowded and attract a wider range of visitors than backcountry.*

BEAR BEHAVIOR	HUMAN RESPONSE
Not aware you're there	Move away without attracting attention.
Aware you're there	Be calm, talk quietly, slowly wave your arms. Move or back away without running.
Approaching	Stand your ground, stay calm, ready your bear spray. Try to **determine the type of approach**. See Chapter 20.
DEFENSIVE APPROACH (the bear is responding to what it perceives as a threat) *Your first response:* Don't threaten; talk in a calm voice, stand still. If the bear stops advancing, slowly move away.	
If the bear keeps approaching	Stand your ground and keep talking.
If the bear seems threatening	Use your bear spray.
If attacked	Fall to the ground and play dead. When the attack stops, lie still and count to 500 to make sure the bear is gone before you move.
OFFENSIVE APPROACH (the bear has not been provoked) *Your first response:* Talk in a firm voice; move out of the bear's path.	
If the bear follows you	Stop, face the bear. Shout and act aggressively. Group together. Try to intimidate the bear. Use your bear spray.
If you're attacked	Fight for your life using anything available.

Adapted from the International Association for Bear Research and Management's "Safety in Bear Country" video.

23

Ready, Aim, Bear Spray

The rolling expanses of Yellowstone National Park's Hayden Valley attract hikers from all over the world. But Kevin and Julie Boyer weren't tourists; they live in nearby Bozeman, Montana, and are experienced outdoors people. They'd even practiced deploying their bear spray in their backyard.

Counter Assault Bear Spray
www.counterassault.com

One day in July 2011 their practice paid off. Kevin later told the *Bozeman Daily Chronicle* that he didn't even remember taking the safety off his can of bear spray. He did remember holding the can with both hands, waiting for the charging female grizzly to get closer. When she stopped Kevin figured it was a bluff charge. But then the cub moved up to its mama's side, and the sow ran full-tilt at Kevin. He had the presence of mind to give a quick spray to the side to test the wind, and then emptied the can, spraying slightly downward to compensate for the spray's tendency to rise on air currents. He remembers watching grizzly bear meet bear spray, feeling as if his life was hanging in the outcome. Her mouth opened, her eyes went wide and then the sow reared up, twisted to the side and ran in the opposite direction.

Rangers later told the Boyers the only thing they did wrong was hiking about ten yards apart; Kevin and Julie say they did that on purpose, just in case something happened to one of them.

Kevin wonders why he meets so many people hiking in prime grizzly country without bear spray. After talking to hundreds of hikers, rangers, and bear experts, I'm pretty sure I know the answer.

The fact that serious bear attacks and fatalities are very rare gives people permission to play the odds. Why spend money just in case? But in this case the answer to "What's the worst thing that can happen?" is sobering. The price of a canister of bear spray (generally between $40 and $50) pales in comparison.

There are countless stories of people who escaped serious injury (or worse) because they were carrying bear spray, and knew how to use it. The U.S. Fish and Wildlife Service says that "bear spray saves lives." The Interagency Grizzly Bear Committee notes, "Bear spray has demonstrated success in fending off charging and attacking bears and preventing, or reducing injury to the person and animal involved." Parks Canada, many U.S. parks, and most bear experts recommend carrying bear spray.

"Dangerous encounters with bears are actually pretty rare, but most wildlife experts recommend carrying a can of bear pepper spray when in the backcountry," says Yellowstone's long-time bear biologist Kerry Gunther. "If other precautionary actions fail, it is a good, last line of defense against an aggressive bear."

Bears are complex individuals, and every bear encounter is unique. Bear spray will not stop 100 percent of bears 100 percent of the time, but carrying and knowing how to use it can improve the odds you'll be able to escape from an aggressive confrontation unharmed.

How Bear Spray Works

Genuine bear spray emits a loud whooshing sound and sprays out a foggy orange cloud of capsaicin and related capsaicinoids—the active irritants in peppers with a heat rating that's off the charts.

Sometimes just the noise plus the sight of the strange orange cloud will send a bear off in the opposite direction. If the bear does keep approaching, once it enters the fog and inhales, misery quickly follows. The potent active ingredients inflame the eyes and lungs, making it difficult for the bear to see or breathe well. Think about what happens if you chop up a red-hot pepper and then accidentally rub your eyes. Now multiply that by 600. Rather than press on with aching lungs and streaming eyes, almost all bears back off.

"Bear spray ain't brains in a can," Dr. Steven French, one of the founders of the Yellowstone Grizzly Foundation, famously quipped many years ago. It's no substitute for common sense, taking proper precautions, and learning how to avoid confrontations with bears. If you travel in bear country, it's your responsibility to learn how to do so safely.

When to Spray

Experts recommend using bear spray when a charging bear is 40 to 50 feet away from you. The expanding cloud of spray should meet the speeding bear when it's about 25 or 30 feet from you. If the bear is not charging, but instead is approaching slowly—as black bears often do—wait until the bear is about 30 feet away to spray.

If you surprise a bear at such close range there's not enough time for it to breathe in the spray before literally running into you, start spraying and keep spraying. The spray may still affect the bear within the next few seconds and cause it to back off, or lessen the severity or duration of the attack. If the bear charges from a distance of 30 feet or closer, the spray must be focused at the front of the bear until it breaks off its charge.

If it's charging from a distance of 30 to 60 feet, spray with a slight side-to-side motion. Spray a couple of three-second bursts, allowing the spray to travel toward the bear, and saving a little in the can in case the bear zig zags or you encounter another bear on your hike out.

Keep Two Hands On the Can

Chuck Bartlebaugh, who runs the Be Bear Aware program, gave cans of bear spray to 50 people and had them aim and spray as though a bear were out in front of them. In most of the tests the force of the propellant coming out caused the can to pivot in their hand, sending the spray up too high to impact a charging bear. That's why Bartlebaugh recommends people use two hands, as Kevin Boyer did, when deploying bear spray.

Practice Makes Perfect

Set up a white target and fire off a half-second burst just to get the feel of it. The oily orange reside will show you where the spray ended up. Mark off distances of 25 feet, 30 feet and 50 feet to give you a visual feeling for distance while your brain is actually working.

Beware of Imposters

The fact that most people who buy bear spray never need to use it has tempted some less than reputable companies to illegally mislabel cheap personal defense sprays and misrepresent them as bear spray. Personal defense, law enforcement, and military sprays, commonly called pepper spray or mace, may work well on humans and canines, but tests show them to be much less effective on bears. The formulas typically contain less potent ingredients and water, so instead of hanging in the air in a cloud, particles quickly drop to the ground. What's your life worth? Because it could depend on your bear spray doing what it's supposed to do. Pepper spray may be cheaper than genuine bear spray, but as is so often the case, you get what you pay for.

How Do You Know It's Bear Spray?

- Always ask for bear spray (not pepper spray) and read the label before you buy.

- By law, all bear sprays must be registered with the EPA and clearly state "for deterring attacks by bears."
- Look for the EPA registration number, the manufacturer's number, and the state or province where the spray is produced.
- Capsaicin and related capsaicinoids should be the active ingredients and be listed as between 1 and 2 percent of the contents. Don't be fooled by claims of 10 – 30 percent oleoresin capsicum—that's not the active ingredient that deters bears.
- Suggested spray duration should be a minimum of 6 seconds to compensate for multiple bears, wind, bears that may zigzag, circle or charge repeatedly, and for the hike out.
- Check the expiration date before you buy.

Bear Spray Isn't Bear Repellent

Don't spray tents, clothes, packs or people. Bear spray is not a repellent, it's a deterrent. And there's some evidence that after it dries, the powerful pepper scent may actually attract bears (see Chapter 15). There is no evidence that bears can smell bear spray in the can, or are attracted to the canister itself.

Cautions

High winds, extreme cold or heat, heavy rain, and dense cover can interfere with the spray. Read the directions carefully so you understand how to make adjustments when conditions are less than ideal.

Grizzly bears that have been sprayed tend to leave the area immediately. Black bears have been known to loiter, which is why experts advise that once the bear's behavior has been deterred, you should leave. See Chapter 21 for more information on how to retreat safely.

Don't store bear spray in direct sunlight in a closed car, or near a heat source like a fire; extreme heat can expand the contents of the can and cause a loss of propellants. Extreme cold can affect performance; try to keep your spray from freezing.

Some agencies report using bear spray successfully on cougars, moose, and elk. Theoretically bear spray would be highly effective on anything with mucous membranes, but it's only been scientifically tested and EPA approved for use as a bear deterrent.

Check local regulations. There are a few parks and other places that classify bear spray as a weapon and prohibit its use.

Where's My Spray?

Carry your spray in a belt or shoulder or chest holster where you can get your hands on it in seconds, not buried in your pack or your jacket pocket. Bears won't patiently stand around waiting while you dig out your bear spray. An extensive review of bear attacks throughout Yellowstone over the past four decades showed that a whopping 79 percent of the hikers attacked were not carrying bear spray. Even worse, a third of the people who were carrying bear spray weren't able to reach it in time to use it.

Traveling With Bear Spray

Bear spray is not allowed on commercial flights in either checked or carry-on luggage. U.S. and Canadian citizens can drive across the border with bear spray for their own personal use, and take it back home again. Bear spray is widely available at sporting goods stores and outdoors stores in bear country. If you hate leaving your expensive bear spray behind when you fly home, you can ship it home via FedEx or UPS. Or if you haven't used it, pay it forward, and give it to an in-bound hiker at the airport. Around Yellowstone National Park you can even recycle your bear spray, thanks to a recycling program developed by Yellowstone Partners.

Bear Spray vs. Bullets

- Steve Herrero's research shows that your chances of being seriously injured by a charging grizzly double when you fire bullets instead of bear spray.
- About half the people who defended themselves with a firearm were injured.
- The majority of the people who defended themselves with bear spray were either not injured at all or had to suffer through shorter attacks that produced less severe injuries. *Source: U.S. Fish and Wildlife Services Fact Sheet No. 8* ❖

Where Did Bear Spray Come From?

Back in the mid-1980s bear biologists, field officers, and other bear experts dreamed about having something that was light and easy to use, effective at a distance of up to 30 feet, and would stop a charging bear in its tracks, without doing any permanent damage to the bear.

Bill Pounds set about making their dreams come true when he developed an ingenious and highly potent pepper-based spray with a unique, expanding-cloud delivery system. Well-respected bear biologist Dr. Chuck Jonkel headed up the clinical and field testing as part of the University of Montana Border Grizzly Project. Over six years of clinical trials and field testing, bear spray proved to be more effective than anyone had hoped, turning away a very high percentage of both black and grizzly bears in over 500 tests. Today the original product Pounds developed is sold under the brand name Counter Assault. I always have a canister on my hip when I hike in bear country.

Making a Difference in Your Community

24

Volunteers for Bears

Volunteers all over North America spend tens of thousands of hours each year working to promote better human-bear relations. My husband Cory Phillips and I were proud members of Colorado's Bear Aware Team for more than a decade.

Volunteers help agencies and parks reach out and take on tasks they just don't have the time, budget or staff to handle. Volunteering gives people a chance to make a real difference. The impact just one

Kids learn the ABC's of being bear smart from Bear Smart Durango's Bryan Peterson.

dedicated and committed person can make is astounding. I could easily write an entire book about volunteers who make the world a better place.

If you're inspired to get involved, chances are there are many opportunities right in your own backyard. A wide range of national organizations have local programs, including Audubon, Defenders of Wildlife, and the National Wildlife Federation. Many national, provincial, state, county and even local parks have active volunteer programs. And many wildlife agencies have discovered that well-trained volunteers can help them stretch their budget and reach people in ways "the government" often cannot.

Bear Aware Teams in Colorado Make a Difference

Colorado's Bear Aware volunteer program started in 1998, after a particularly challenging summer when district wildlife managers did nothing but handle bear calls—and felt that despite all their efforts, they weren't affecting any real changes in human behavior.

The Division of Wildlife (now Colorado Parks and Wildlife) already had a very strong volunteer program. So they decided to recruit people who were interested in bears and train them to help their neighbors understand what causes conflicts and how to avoid them.

Today hundreds of volunteers have gone through Bear Aware training and have played important roles in many of the state's bear success stories. Armed with bear kits, presentations, and a library full of literature, activities, videos, handouts, and giveaways, more than 200 Bear Aware volunteers on 20 teams across the state work with their communities to inform, inspire, and motivate people to live more responsibly and prevent problems with bears. That gives wildlife officers time to do all those things volunteers cannot.

Bear Aware teams partner with their area's district wildlife managers and tackle jobs that range from canvasing neighborhoods with handouts to staffing booths at events and giving presentations. Many Bear Aware volunteers also make house calls, helping people identify things that might be attracting bears and offering practical ways to solve their problems. As many agencies know, one of the reasons people who are having problems don't call sooner is that they fear the agency is going to come and kill the bear. Focus groups and research shows that people are much less wary of calling a neighbor who is a volunteer, even though they represent the agency.

"Because issues with bears are largely a community issue, it is imperative members of the community are involved in recognizing what is attracting bears to their neighborhoods and then taking action to minimize those attractants and solve their problems," said Mary McCormac, one of the Education and Watchable Wildlife Coordinators for Colorado Parks and Wildlife. "I can understand agency reluctance to engage volunteers, as the care and feeding of volunteers takes a fair amount of personnel time and commitment. But it is impossible for an agency with limited staff and resources to respond to every issue, participate in every event, and present to every group in hopes of encouraging people to live responsibly with bears and other wildlife. Volunteers are critical in providing community outreach and education in areas where conflicts with bears is a consistent issue, which helps free-up our wildlife officers' time to focus on human safety concerns or other pressing matters."

The unbridled joy of learning, straight from the bear's mouth. *© Donna Forrest*

Bake a Pie, Save a Bear

Back in the 1800s homesteaders planted orchards in what is today Yosemite National Park. Apple trees are persistent and hardy, and the valley is now home to rare varieties of heirloom apples like Spitzenberg, Winesap, King, and Northern Spy. Bears go bonkers for apples, and the remnant orchards can create big problems come fall. So every year Yosemite organizes an apple picking event in Curry Village in late July or early August (check the Park's website) and invites all visitors, volunteers, and staff to collect and take home apples. Proactive programs like this one help keep bears away from developed areas and focused on natural food sources.

Bears Get Under Your Skin

One thing that really struck me as I was pulling together stories and tidbits for this revised edition was the amazing longevity, determination and persistence of so many of the people who spend every day of their lives promoting peaceful coexistence and educating humans about how to reduce conflicts and solve problems. Thirty, forty even fifty years of dedicated service is not uncommon.

Why are so many people willing to spend most of their lives figuratively beating their heads against a wall of ignorance, indifference and apathy? Because that's the only way that wall will ever crumble. Another chapter in the history of human-bear relations is currently being written; how it turns out is up to all of us. ❖

Signs of Change at Crystal Lakes

Crystal Lakes is a picture-perfect private community on 5,000 wooded acres in the middle of Roosevelt National Forest in northern Colorado. There are 1,600 properties, 800 homes and about the same number of seasonal campers and trailers. Most residents are part-timers. The story of the problems they created for the area's bears is a common one. The way the community partnered with Colorado Parks and Wildlife to solve their problem is not.

In the 1990s Crystal Lakes had a dirty little secret. People liked to watch bears. Some people fed them and nobody minded too much if they visited the dump. But when the dump was fenced, bears started breaking into campers in the storage yard searching for food. At first people shrugged it off, but eventually bears graduated to breaking

© Curt Livingston

into homes; soon a hundred or more break-ins a year were costing about $150,000. No one told Parks and Wildlife, because they didn't want them to come kill the bears.

Finally one fed-up resident talked to the media, the story made the Denver news and then got picked up by the Associated Press. And the community finally admitted they had a serious problem and reached out for help. CPW had started their Bear Aware volunteer program in 1998, but there was no team in Crystal. Long-time district wildlife manager Jim Jackson was worried about getting volunteers involved in managing "his" bears. But he was scraping the bottom of his big box of bear-ideas, and agreed to give volunteers a try.

Of course, it wasn't the bears that needed to be managed. After a series of community meetings the Crystal Lakes Bear Aware Team was started in mid-summer 2005. They quickly went to work meeting with neighbors, setting up patrols and a phone tree, handing out bear literature, and attending new owner orientations. But bears were hungry, hyperphagia was right around the corner, and change doesn't happen overnight.

After a string of home break-ins, a bear was trapped at the scene. Bear Aware volunteer Jim Tiffin sat with the caged bear until the officer could get there to kill him. Both officer and volunteer ended up in tears at the death of this healthy bear in his prime.

The volunteer was a seasoned hunter who was surprised by his emotional reaction. Visit my website to read his thoughtful essay published in the first edition of this book.

© Jim Tiffin

Remorse led to determination. The Crystal Team grew and committed themselves to making sure the community didn't kill any more bears. Crystal Lakes now discourages feeding birds and encourages residents to bear-proof. Unwelcome mats, portable electric fences, and other deterrents are used to keep bears out. Over the years they've come up with some innovative ways to remind people why they need to be bear smart.

When team organizers Jim and Jane Tiffin saw a silhouette bear in a little town in Texas, a big light bulb went off. Here was the creative, clever way to keep people bear aware that they'd been searching for. Making the sign was easy. Convincing the HOA board it was a good idea to put it up was a little harder. But the community got behind it, the sign went up, and bear problems went down.

When the sign was first installed, one realtor called it the Realtor Eradication Program. That same realtor now says that the program and sign give Crystal Lakes a competitive advantage over neighboring communities.

The team leaders who started the Bear Aware program have moved out of the community, but the team goes on. And community managers promise that Crystal Lakes will stay bear smart. ❖

© Jim Tiffin

25

Partnering Up for Bears

Whose Bears Are They, Anyway?

"Come get your bear," is a plea frequently heard by bear managers. It generally originates from people experiencing problems with bears who want the bear hauled away to "where it belongs." Under those circumstances, most agencies are all too happy to point out that bears don't belong to them, they belong to all of us. But bear managers can get quite defensive when "outsiders" express opinions on how to

© *Paul Conrad*

deal with problems, or angrily insist "don't you dare hurt our bear." Perhaps it's like your kids; you can criticize them all you want, but let someone else go after them, and they'll have one angry and defensive mama and papa to deal with.

For Better or For Worse

Natural resources belong to us all. They're not ours to enjoy when we feel like it and someone else's to take care of. Taking ownership and sharing responsibility is the first step to building bridges that lead to better human-bear relations.

Jaime Sajecki, Virginia's Black Bear Project Leader, is a big believer in community involvement. "We interviewed Virginians for our educational video on living in bear country. Having real people from your area talking about their bear experiences is key; everyone thinks their own situation is unique and 'some hippie bear-hugger or city-folk from somewhere else' couldn't possibly understand. Our message revolves around the idea that bears belong to everyone in the Commonwealth of Virginia; they are not the property of the Virginia Department of Game and Inland Fisheries or any one person. It is everyone's responsibility to prevent problems with bears so that we can continue to enjoy having such a wonderful native wildlife species in the state. This is such an important value that it was incorporated into our most recent 10-year bear management plan by our public stakeholders' advisory committee. We seize every opportunity to hammer home the personal responsibility message."

Lake City Friends of the Bears—A Partnership That Works

There are a variety of reasons why non-profits working for bears can't or don't partner up with the wildlife agency responsible for bear management. Some agencies really discourage "outside involvement." Others have policies that non-profits disagree with. I have talked to hundreds of bear folks from both agencies and organizations, and have come to believe that in most cases partnering and working together is the most productive way to improve human-bear relations, and make any long-term changes that are needed.

Lake City Friends of the Bears in Colorado is run by Patrice and Craig Palmer, who are also Bear Aware volunteers for Colorado Parks and Wildlife. Here's what their District Wildlife Manager, Lucas Martin, had to say: "They have been trained by me to set up pepper spray barrels, work on community outreach, and even have their own Bear Day in the town park during the 4th of July celebrations. They help with education programs at local schools, moose captures, bear releases, and have even developed place mats for local restaurants with bear messaging on them. They continue to come up with amazing ideas and ways to mitigate wildlife conflict. We have a fantastic working relationship and they really deserve huge thanks."

Town of Snowmass Village—A Community Effort

About 2,800 people live year-round in the Town of Snowmass Village, tucked into the picture-postcard splendor of Colorado's Roaring Fork Valley. Snowmass is a four-season high-country mecca that attracts an endless stream of visitors. There are festivals, events, and happenings most weekends. It's a prime vacation destination. It's also prime bear habitat.

Laurie Smith, who's been with Animal Services for longer than she can remember and Tina White, who joined the team in 1997, share a phone, an office and a passion: arming people with the information and motivation they need to share space with the bears that lived there long before the first mountain men arrived. With the full

This sticker reminds people that whether or not the dumpster is actually bear-resistant depends on whether or not they take ten seconds to latch it.

support of Snowmass' eight police officers, who have all been trained in the causes and prevention of problems as well as how to respond to immediate issues, and long-time District Wildlife Manager Kevin Wright, there's a trained professional on-call to deal with human-bear conflicts 24/7.

The town's tough anti-feeding ordinance (patterned after West Yellowstone, Montana) was enacted back in 1994. Residents must secure trash in bear-resistant containers; store it inside a home, garage or enclosure that's been inspected and approved by the police department; and wait until the morning of pickup to take trash to the curb. It's illegal to intentionally or unintentionally feed wildlife. Bird feeders must be suspended out of reach on sturdy cables and the area beneath must be kept clean of hulls and seeds. The ordinance has been strengthened and revised a couple of times since then to give officers the ability to write tickets and levy hefty fines. The ability to make people literally pay for their offenses provides leverage, but the team would much rather have the person invest in a bear-resistant container than pay a fine.

"Everyone seems to pattern their ordinance after Snowmass," says Kevin Wright. "They decided they did not want to have any more bears put down due to human error, and took responsibility for where they chose to live and build their town. They got council and citizen support. It works." (You'll find the Snowmass ordinance, and others on *www.LivingWithBears.com*.)

Bear Response Contractors

Florida's unique Bear Response Contractor Program is so successful it's now a line item in the Florida Fish and Wildlife Conservation Commission's budget and no longer relies on grants for funding. There are 15 contractors statewide, with at least one in each of five regions. The contractors are trained by FWC to handle and respond to routine bear calls.

Annual Bear Festival in Florida Takes Cooperation Times Six

A state agency, a county, a city, the feds, a national wildlife organization, and a scenic byway all team up for bears in Florida. The Florida Black Bear and Wildlife Conservation Festival started in 1999 as part of a concerted effort to reach out and encourage Floridians to learn more about bears. About 5,000 people trek to Umatilla, Florida, in the heart of Ocala National Forest each year for this popular one-day event that's so much fun people hardly notice they're learning something.

The festival features interactive programs, field trips, information booths, exhibits and live entertainment. People can learn about camping safety, have their photo taken with Smokey Bear, go on a guided field trip into black bear habitat, and have questions answered by bear biologists. This family-oriented event features lots of activities for children, including the popular "Come Be a Bear," where kids don furry vests and take an interactive journey to discover how bears find food and survive in the wild. This long-lived festival is a great example of the power of collaboration. It's put on each year by a coalition of agencies and other organizations that all work together and get it done. Current sponsors include the City of Umatilla, the FWC, the U.S. Forest Service, the Black Bear Scenic Byway, Defenders of Wildlife and the Lake County Commission.

Education and fun at the Florida Black Bear Festival. *US Forest Service*

Air Force Goes Bear Friendly

"We were the McDonald's for bears," said Colonel Curt Van De Walle, Commander of the 1st Special Operations Mission Support Group at Hurlburt Air Field in Okaloosa County, Florida. The base is surrounded by bear habitat, but the resident bears quickly learned it was much easier to drop by and eat on base. Hurlburt converted all of their trash containers to bear-resistant models and started a rigorous education program on living in bear country for everyone who lives or works on base. Florida Fish and Wildlife Conservation Commission (FWC) trained their security forces on how to respond properly to bears, including administering aversive conditioning. After a year of efforts, conflicts on the base dropped by 70 percent and FWC honored Hurlburt for being a "Bear Safe Community."

© Kristal Walsh

Rent-A-Can: Save Your Dinner and Your Bears

The High Parks Wilderness in the Adirondack backcountry has long been a hub of human-bear interactions, many of which could charitably be described as "negative" for both people and bears. Research showed that the number of interactions increased in direct proportion to the number of visitors to the popular hiking and camping area.

Predictably, most incidents revolve around bears trying to get people food. In addition to all the usual sources (unsecured coolers, food left in vehicles or campsites) bears in the area had come to regard bear bags—food stored in a stuff sack and hung in a tree—as a reliable food source.

The clever cable system that works so well in Great Smoky Mountains National Park didn't solve the problems in High Parks. Studies showed that the failure was due to a combination of improper hardware, few suitable locations, and campers overloading the cables, all of which contributed to bears learning how to use the cables to reel in a big food prize.

The Wildlife Conservation Society (WCS) determined there were several contributing factors: people were not very aware of bears or how their actions impacted them and their own safety and comfort; because people didn't know much about bears, they weren't very tolerant; and reliable methods of bear-proofing food weren't widely available in the wilderness.

Eventually the WCS partnered with the New York Department of Environmental Conservation and set about making bear-resistant canisters more widely available to campers and backpackers. WCS purchased and distributed canisters to retail stores throughout the state. The stores rented out the canisters and educated users about the benefits of keeping their food safe from bears.

Ultimately New York adopted state regulations requiring the use of commercially manufactured bear canisters in the eastern High Peaks from April 1 to November 30. Ongoing research and studies about the most effective communication systems further refined efforts.

Soon the combined efforts were paying off. Human bear interactions dropped from a high of 420 in 2004 to fewer than 100 in 2007 as people got the message. ❖

Evolution of a Bear Smart Community

Whistler, British Columbia is a four-season mecca for outdoor enthusiasts of all persuasions, from skiers and boarders to hikers, mountain bikers and runners to people who simply enjoy the great outdoors. Whistler's approximately 10,000 permanent residents are a drop in the bucket compared to 11,500 seasonal homeowners, 2,500 seasonal workers, and two million annual visitors.

No one knows how many bears once inhabited these lush mountain valleys. Today 50–60 black bears are doing their best to share space with a booming human population. Between 1988 and 1998 Whistler's population grew 13 percent a year, swelling from just over 4,000 people to more than 10,000. By 2014 the number of human-bear interactions had increased manyfold, but the number of bears killed as a result of human-caused conflict has been cut almost in half. Why? Because bear smart behavior has slowly become a way of life in Whistler.

In 2011 after more than a decade of efforts spearheaded by the Whistler Bear Working Group (see the Get Bear Smart Society story) to educate, inspire, and implement bear smart practices, Whistler was officially recognized for meeting a long list of tough requirements and designated a Bear Smart Community. Whistler is now one of seven Bear Smart Communities in British Columbia that are proving that committed communities can coexist with bears.

No one has ever been killed by a bear in Whistler. But every year in the province of British Columbia an average of 824 black bears and

48 grizzlies are killed by conservation officers as a result of human-caused problems or perceived "threats" to human safety. The Resort Municipality of Whistler seems determined to keep its bears safe, and has enacted a variety of bylaws and practices designed to keep people from attracting bears into residential and commercial areas.

Whistler has no curbside garbage pickup. Single-family homeowners are required to drop off waste, recycling and compost at a bear-proof depot. Businesses and multi-unit residential complexes use commercial operators to pick up waste from mandated bear-resistant bins or enclosures. There are bear-proof garbage bins along the sidewalks. An electric fence surrounds the waste transfer station.

The landfill's journey to being bear-proofed highlights the ingenuity and persistence of both bears and people. As a first step, the municipal landfill was completely enclosed by an electric fence. To avoid being zapped and still get to that garbage treasure-trove, the bears dove into the landfill from nearby trees and rock piles. They climbed wooden fence posts. They dug under the fence. They scooted through the gate if it was left open. Some even made a mad dash between the wires.

Determined to outsmart the bears, the town installed concrete barriers to keep them from digging under and installed a cleverly

© Sylvia Dolson

designed gate with plastic handles, so the power is always on. All the trees inside the landfill were removed, so if a bear did manage to get in, there was nowhere to hide.

The final touch was an electrified cattle grate that people and trucks could safely pass over, but delivered a big shock to bear feet. Now and then a particularly determined and enlightened bear figured out a way in (maybe they jumped into a truck and hid out), but most gave up the assault and resumed foraging on natural foods.

Popular landscaping plants that provide bear food like mountain ash, clover, blueberries, and huckleberries are discouraged for residential planting, and no longer permitted in landscapes requiring municipal approval.

Today the Whistler Bear Working Group labors tirelessly (O.K., sometimes they get tired...but they keep working anyway) to ensure that Whistler continues to incorporate and improve the long-term bear smart practices and outstanding educational programs that

have proved so successful in reducing human-bear conflicts and ensuring that bears and humans can continue to share and enjoy their mountain home.

For more and the criteria for becoming a Bear Smart community, please visit: *www.whistler.ca* and *www.getbearsmart.com.*

© Sylvia Dolson

How Whistler Makes It Work

- Violators of Whistler's bear-smart bylaws and ordinances can face fines up to $2,000. Serious offenders can find themselves in court, facing a $10,000 fine and three months in jail.
- Bear-resistant waste containers or enclosures are mandatory.
- Backyard composting is discouraged; public composting bins accept food waste and sell the rich organic soil it produces.
- Fruits and berries must be harvested regularly and fallen fruit removed from the ground.
- Bird feeders must be inaccessible to bears.
- Garbage containers for special events must be picked up and emptied by 10 p.m. ❖

"We love our bears, yet we know that giving them what they love—our food—will likely result in their death. If we don't spoil them with human contact and human food, bears can live peacefully in the surrounding area. They wander the same forests, den on our ski hill, and devour the flowers we photograph. And although they have the power to cause serious harm, they choose not to." — *Sylvia Dolson, Get Bear Smart Society*

BLACK BEAR POPULATIONS BY STATE / PROVINCE

State	2015 Black Bear Population	Human-Bear Conflicts/Yr	Conflict Bears Killed/Yr	Conflict Trend
Alabama	125–225	31	1	Up
Alaska	100,000	1,133	27	Stable
Arizona	1,500–2,500	18	18	Stable
Arkansas	4,000–5,000	410	3	Up
California **	35,000	259	74	Stable
Colorado	18,000	N/A	275	N/A
Connecticut	500–700	442	2	Up
Florida	3,000+	5,584	22	Up
Georgia	5,100	1,488	7	Up
Idaho	27,000	≤ 100	≤25	Stable
Kentucky	500–700	386	6	Up
Louisiana	500–800	246	2	Up
Maine	31,000+	555	12	Up
Maryland	1,000+	337	4	Down
Massachusetts	4,000–5,000	145	5	Up
Michigan	11,000	250	1	Stable
Minnesota	12,000–14,000	640	20	Stable
Mississippi	150–200	50	0	Up
Missouri	300	8	0	Up
Montana	13,307	N/A	177	Varies greatly
Nevada	600	402	≤6	Up
New Hampshire	5,300	698	14	Stable
New Jersey	3,500	2,612	33	Up
New Mexico	6,000–8,000	368	120	Stable
New York	6,000–8,000	768	29	Stable
North Carolina	18,000–20,500	587	10	Up
Ohio	50–100	18	0	Stable
Oklahoma *	*250*	N/A	N/A	N/A
Oregon	25,000	483	361	Varies greatly
Pennsylvania	18,000	2,112	33	Up
Rhode Island	0–10	6	0	Up
South Carolina	800–1,200	290	2	Stable

State	2015 Black Bear Population	Human-Bear Conflicts/Yr	Conflict Bears Killed/Yr	Conflict Trend
South Dakota	unknown	N/A	N/A	N/A
Tennessee	4,800	428	15	Stable
Texas	300	5	0	Variable
Utah	4,100	65	89	Up
Vermont	5,000–6,000	533	18	Stable
Virginia	17,000	838	3	Up
Washington ***	25,000	529	250	Stable
West Virginia	10,000–12,000	946	80	Up
Wisconsin	22,620	1,105	12	Down
Wyoming *	*2,500–4,500*	154	≤22	Stable
CANADA				
Alberta ****	40,000	2,532	162	Stable
British Columbia	120,000–160,000	N/A	N/A	N/A
Manitoba *****	25,000–35,000	1,456	168	Down
New Brunswick	17,000	200+	N/A	Up
Newfoundland	6,000–10,000	N/A	N/A	Up
Northwest Territory*	*5,000+*	N/A	N/A	N/A
Nova Scotia	10,000	471	22	Stable
Ontario	85,000–105,000	5,813	164	Variable
Quebec	71,000–83,000	738	137	Stable
Saskatchewan*	*24,000*	N/A	N/A	N/A
Yukon	10,000	47	172	Up

Population estimates, human-bear conflicts 2009–2014, and conflict trend as reported on the 2015 agency surveys completed for the IBA's 2015 Black Bear Workshops for Eastern and Western North America. British Columbia estimate from Ministry of the Environment. Annual human-bear conflicts are mean (midpoint) numbers; conflict bears killed are annual average numbers, both calculated over 5 years.

* Population numbers from 2005; new data not provided.

** Number of depredation permits issued that allow the property owner to kill the bear or hire someone to do so. An average of 41% of permits issued result in a bear being killed.

*** 200 of the bears were killed under timber damage depredation permits issued to lumber producers that allow them to kill bears damaging commercial trees.

**** Conflicts includes sightings.

***** Conflicts are down 17% since implementing Bear Smart Program.

WHERE TO SEE BEARS

You can easily watch grizzly bears in natural habitats at the Grizzly and Wolf Discovery Center in Montana. There are also many places in the U.S. and Canada where you have a good chance of seeing black bears and/or grizzly bears in the wild. Chapter 19 has guidelines on how to safely view and photograph bears.

Grizzly & Wolf Discovery Center
www.grizzlydiscoveryctr.com
This not-for-profit wildlife park in West Yellowstone, Montana, is a good place to see bears and other wildlife up close. They offer a wide variety of daily programs, including a very special opportunity for kids to help hide food for the grizzlies to discover, demonstrations on how to use bear spray, plus a terrific museum. There are eight working grizzly bears and six wolves in natural habitats, plus several raptors. Check the website for programs, exhibits and hours. Also home to the Interagency Grizzly Bear Container Product Testing Program.

Alaska
www.wildlifeviewing.alaska.gov
Extensive information about bear viewing opportunities within the state, including virtual viewing opportunities via trail cams, web cams and live feeds. Download guides and order publications.

Search Tips: Go to the Park's website and search black bears. An independent search of the park's name + black bears often yields more information. Many have lotteries and/or require permits, so plan ahead.

Several sites have been developed specifically for bear viewing, including Anan Creek (Wrangell), Fish Creek (Hyder), Margaret Creek (Ketchikan), Pack Creek (Juneau).

Some suggestions include:

Denali National Park
Kodiak National Wildlife Refuge
McNeil River State Game Sanctuary and Refuge (permit lottery)
Katmai National Park (Brooks Camp/Brooks Lodge)
Tongass National Forest

California
Yosemite National Park

Montana
Glacier National Park

North Carolina
Alligator River National Wildlife Refuge
Pocosin Lakes National Wildlife Refuge (called the "American Serengeti")

Tennessee
Great Smoky Mountains National Park

Wyoming
Yellowstone National Park

Canada

Canadian Provincial Parks

Canadian National Parks
www.pc.gc.ca
Banff
Jasper
Yoho
Kootenay
Waterton Lakes (adjacent to Glacier)

BEAR ORGANIZATIONS

Bear Smart Community Program:

British Columbia, Canada
www.env.gov.bc.ca/wld/bearsmart/

Alberta, Canada
http://esrd.alberta.ca/recreation-public-use/alberta-bear-smart/
A voluntary program that encourages communities, businesses and individuals to work together to prevent human-bear conflicts, reduce risks to human safety and private property, and reduce the number of bears killed each year. Communities must meet a series of criteria to earn the "Bear Smart" designation. Criteria, case histories, brochures and more info available on the website. Program was designed by the Ministry of Water, Land and Air Protection in partnership with the British Columbia Conservation Foundation and the Union of British Columbia Municipalities.

Bear Smart Durango
www.bearsmartdurango.org
Founded in 2000 by Bryan Peterson, Bear Smart Durango is a non-profit group that has steadily grown into a widely-respected organization dedicated to education, outreach and conflict prevention with an impressive board of scientific and real-world advisors. Education Director Cindy Lawrence brings more than 20 years of experience as a wildlife biologist with the U.S. Forest Service to the organization. Excellent, informative and easy-to-navigate website with many resources and links. Headquartered in Durango, Colorado.

Be Bear Aware Classroom on Wheels
bearinfo@cwfi.org
The Be Bear Aware Campaign is an outreach program under the direction of Chuck Bartlebaugh that emphasizes bear safety and stewardship in bear country. They work directly with schools, youth groups, hunters, fishermen, outfitters, guides, and backcountry horsemen. Their educational events include training the trainers on bear safety and avoidance. Their classroom on wheels covers the entire Northwest and includes bear mounts, displays, educational panels, brochures, and bear avoidance coloring books. Reach Be Bear Aware at 406-239-2315.

Bow Valley Wildsmart
www.wildsmart.ca/bearsmart
The WildSmart program is a pro-active coalition of community members, government entities, environmental organizations and businesses with a goal of reducing human-bear conflicts in Alberta's Bow Valley through education and outreach, attractant management and bear management. Extensive resources and links on the website.

Get Bear Smart Society
www.bearsmart.com
The comprehensive and in-depth website for this Canadian non-profit is widely regarded as one of the best resources for information on coexisting with bears and preventing human-bear conflicts. Resources, links and educational materials for download. Bear Smart Playing Cards and several books for sale.

International Association for Bear Research and Management (IBA)
www.bearbiology.com
For all species of bears worldwide. IBA hosts national and international conferences, publishes quarterly newsletters, and *Ursus*, the professional journal for bear and bear management issues. Back issues on the website.

Living with Wildlife Foundation
www.lwwf.org
While funding for the Living with Wildlife Foundation was unavailable as this book went to press, their well-respected guides (see Recommended Reading section) are currently still available for download. The Foundation's equally well-respected director Patti Sowka has migrated over to the private sector as a conflict prevention specialist, but she continues to work with other wildlife professionals to prevent human-bear conflicts through her involvement with the International Union for Conservation of Nature (IUCN) Bear Specialist Group as a member of the Human Bear Conflict Expert Team. Reach Patti Sowka at 406-544-5307 or psowka15@gmail.com.

Sierra Wild
www.sierrawild.gov
A joint-effort website of the US Forest Service, National Park Service, and Bureau of Land Management. These three agencies manage more than two dozen designated wilderness areas along the spine of the Sierra Nevada, and are aiming to make recreating in bear country and complying with the areas varying regulations regarding food storage a bit easier. Besides bear info, the website lists approved bear canisters and shows areas where canisters are required by law.

WildSafe BC British Columbia Conservation Foundation
https://wildsafebc.com/black-bear/
More extensive information and much easier to find than info on the Ministry of Environment website.

Wind River Bear Institute
www.beardogs.org
Bear shepherding using Karelian Bear Dogs, under directorship of Carrie Hunt. Works with individuals, agencies and communities in the U.S., Canada and internationally. In addition to KBDs, they offer seminars, training and workshops. Headquartered in Montana.

WILDLIFE INFORMATION & ORGANIZATIONS

Colorado State University
www.coopext.colostate.edu/wildlife/bears.html
The Cooperative Extension Office has a wide variety of brochures about agriculture, horticulture, livestock and beekeeping.

Cornell University Cooperative Extension Office
www.cce.cornell.edu
Research, informational brochures.

Defenders of Wildlife
www.defenders.org
Primarily involved with threatened and endangered species; does a lot of cooperative programs for grizzly bears and polar bears.

The Humane Society of the United States
www.hsus.org

Interagency Grizzly Bear Committee
www.igbconline.org
In-depth information and links to further resources on living and recreating in grizzly bear country, including advice on safely viewing bears. To find bear-resistant containers that have passed the center's testing protocol, look under Safety in Grizzly Country and then Bear-Resistant Products for a current list.

National Audubon Society
www.audubon.org

National Wildlife Federation
www.nwf.org

BEAR-RESISTANT PRODUCT TESTING

Grizzly & Wolf Discovery Center
www.grizzlydiscoveryctr.com
Located in West Yellowstone, Montana, the Center is the only facility approved for testing products for the IGBC bear-resistant products program. The testing procedures were developed in cooperation with the Forest Service; Montana Fish, Wildlife and Parks; Living with Wildlife Foundation; and the Interagency Grizzly Bear Committee. Protocol for having products tested is on the website. The list of products that pass the tests can be found at: *www.igbconline.org*

SAMPLE COMMUNITY ORDINANCES

Wildlife ordinances from West Yellowstone, Montana; the Town of Snowmass Village, Colorado; and Hemlock Farms, Pennsylvania, are posted on our website at *www.LivingWith Bears.com*

BOOKS, DVDS, GUIDES, CURRICULUMS

Books

Backcountry Bear Basics, Dave Smith

Bear, Daniel J. Cox and Rebecca L. Grambo

Bear-ology: Fascinating Bear Facts, Tales & Trivia, Sylvia Dolson

Bear Attacks: Their Causes and Avoidance, Updated 2nd Edition, Stephen Herrero

Bear Aware, Bill Schneider

Bear in the Backseat I & II, Kim DeLozier and Carolyn Jourdan

Bears: Monarchs of the Northern Wilderness, Wayne Lynch

The Bears of Yellowstone, Paul Schullery

Bears Without Fear, Kevin Van Tighem

Black Bear Country, Michael Furtman

The Great Bear Almanac, Gary Brown

Great Colorado Bear Stories, Laura Pritchett

Great Montana Bear Stories, Benjamin Long

Great Wyoming Bear Stories, Tom Reed

The Grizzly Maze: Timothy Treadwell's Fatal Obsession with Alaskan Bears, Nick Jans

Joy of Bears, Sylvia Dolson

Mark of the Grizzly, Updated 2nd Edition, Scott McMillion

Mountain Bears, Wayne Lynch

Safe Travel in Bear Country, Gary Brown

A Shadow in the Forest: Idaho's Black Bear, John Beecham and John Rohlman

Speaking of Bears: The Bear Crisis and a Tale of Rewilding from Yosemite, Sequoia and Other National Parks, Rachel Mazur

A Whistler Bear Story, Sylvia Dolson

Yellowstone Bears in the Wild, James Halfpenny

Books for Kids

The Adventures of Baby Bear, Aubrey Lang & Wayne Lynch

Bear-ly There, Rebekah Raye

Bear Smart Kids, Evelyn Kirkaldy (from *www.bearsmart.com*)

If You Were a Bear, Rachel Mazur

The Troublesome Cub in the Great Smoky Mountains, Lisa Horstman

Videos & DVDs

Safety in Bear Country Society
The following three videos DVDs are endorsed by the International Association for Bear Research and Management (IBA), and contain the consensus opinions of the leading experts on living, working and recre-

ating in bear country. Steve Herrero consulted on their production. Available from Distribution Access, *www.distributionaccess.com*

Living in Bear Country
Practical advice on ways people and communities can make simple adjustments that can reduce property damage and increase human safety. Covers living responsibly and safely with black bears and grizzly bears.

Staying Safe in Bear Country
Provides information designed to help reduce human injuries and property damage from black and grizzly bears throughout North America. Lots of information on bear behavior and advice on preventing bear encounters and attacks. Available in English and French.

Working in Bear Country
Provides in-depth information on field safety, including employee responsibilities, camp safety, including location and design, attractant management, bear detection and deterrent systems, firearms, bear response planning (a companion video to *Staying Safe in Bear Country*). Available in English and French.

Guides

Living with Wildlife Foundation
The following guides are available for download from *www.lwwf.org*

Recreating in Bear, Wolf and Mountain Lion Country. Products and techniques, bear-resistant backpacking containers for food and garbage storage, hanging food and gear, portable electric fencing, outfitters' panniers, much more.

Techniques and Refuse Management Options for Residential Areas, Campgrounds, and Group-Use Facilities. Bear-resistant containers, refuse and recycling centers, other products and methods for securing and storing garbage, livestock feed, pet food and other attractants, methods for deterring predators including electric fencing, scaring predators from your property.

Electric Fencing Guide. Contains information on electric fencing designs that can be used to help deter predators including bears, mountain lions and wolves.

Predator Behavior and Modification Tools (for wildlife professionals only). Deterring, aversively conditioning and trapping predators. Not available on the website; contact Patti Sowka directly: call 406-544-5307 or email psowka15@gmail.com.

Educational Resources

The Florida Black Bear Curriculum Guide
myfwc.com/education/educators/
This outstanding, beautifully illustrated 193-page guide is a comprehensive series of lessons on the natural history and conservation needs of Florida's black bear and is designed to educate and stimulate teachers and students in grades 3-8. While the guide focuses on Florida's black bear, it contains lots of creative activities as well as great ideas for engaging students. A joint project of FWC and Defenders of Wildlife.

Understanding Black Bears, K-8 Classroom Curriculum

www.blackbearinfo.com

As part of its continuing effort to educate New Jersey residents about coexisting with black bears, the NJ-DEP Division of Fish and Wildlife partnered with state wildlife agencies in New York, Florida and Arkansas, the New Jersey State Federation of Sportsmen's Clubs, and Untamed Science to produce the "Understanding Black Bears" K-8 curriculum and education website. Free multimedia resources for teachers and students include movies, images, quizzes, puzzles, computer games, and tons of interactive learning within 29 lesson activities and related classroom support materials.

Project WILD K-12 Program

http://ProjectWILD.org

Project WILD activity guides and materials include a lot of information about bears (*Bearly Born, How Many Bears Can Live in This Forest?* and *What Bear Goes Where?)* as well as other wildlife and wild resources. Project WILD also hosts educators' workshops around the country.

Black Bear Ecology Teacher's Guide

http://bears.mnr.gov.on.ca/

Designed by the Ministry of Natural Resources for Ontario, Canada, in cooperation with Ontario Bearwise, these teacher guides for grades 2, 4 and 7 include background reading, activities, lesson plans, recommended resources, and *Are You Bearwise?* ebook.

Wild About Bears! An Educator's Activity Guide

www.wildbc.org

This unique guide for educators working with children grades K-7 uses bears and other environmental-related topics as organizing concepts in teaching to allow students to reach a deeper understanding so they can apply their knowledge to the real world. It contains a conceptual framework, key concept overview, primer, and activities.

Grizzly Bears Forever!

http://cpaws.org

A teacher activity guide for Science 7, 8 and 9, available from Canadian Parks and Wilderness (CPAWS). Also available from Friends of Banff National Park. CPAWS is a national charity that works collaboratively with governments, local communities, industry and indigenous peoples to protect Canada's amazing natural places and natural resources, including wildlife.

WSPA Bears of the World: Fact sheets and Education activities

www.worldanimalprotection.us.org

Specifically developed for use in schools, ages 9-14, this resource contains a series of information sheets on the eight bear species and a Bear Facts booklet, as well as a full-color "Bears of the World" wall chart that provides information about the natural lives of the world's eight bear species, the threats they face, and ways in which humans can help to safeguard their habitats and their welfare. Published by the World Society for the Protection of Animals.

DETERRENTS

Bear Spray

Beware of imposters. The EPA registration number is required to be shown on the front label of registered bear-deterrent sprays (available in sporting goods stores or online). As of May 2015, the list includes:

Counter Assault Bear Deterrent
www.counterassault.com

Guard Alaska Bear Repellent
McNeil River Enterprises

UDAP Pepper Power Bear Deterrent Spray
www.PepperPower.com

Frontiersman Bear Attack Deterrent
www.sabre-sabrered.com

Electronic Watchdogs

Rex Plus, the Electronic Watchdog detects motion through doors, walls and windows up to 30 feet away, and barks realistically. On and off switch, adjustable volume. Not bear specific—will also bark at people, deer, dogs and other medium-sized mammals. Visit *www.sti-usa.com* or search the Internet to find retailer or distributor.

Electric Fencing

In addition to the companies listed below, good instructions can be downloaded from state agency websites, including Colorado, Virginia and Montana. Some states will help with installation or loan out temporary fences.

Gallagher North America
www.am.gallagher.com

Kencove Farm Fence
www.kencove.com

J.L. Williams
www.safefence.com

Premier1Supplies
www.premier1supplies.com

Portable and Camping Fences
USFS Tested and Approved Chargers and Portable Mesh Systems (2007) is a 10-page Recreation Tech Tips bulletin from the Forest Service Technology and Development Program. It includes detailed instructions and lists all approved energizers and portable mesh fence systems that passed lab and field testing. Find a PDF on *www.LivingWithBears.com.*

Protecting Beehives/Apiaries
www.dgif.virginia.gov/wildlife/bear/fencing.pdf
Search your state/province name + "protecting apiaries from black bears" for area-specific designs and programs. For detailed info on specs and installation, see electric fence manufacturers' websites.

Electric Fence Guide
www.lwwf.org
Contains information on electric fencing designs that can be used to help deter predators including bears, mountain lions and wolves.

GOVERNMENT AGENCIES

U.S. National Parks
www.nps.gov

U.S. Fish & Wildlife Services
www.fws.gov

U.S. Forest Service
www.fs.fed.us
Search: Watchable Wildlife + black bear

U.S. State Wildlife Management Agencies

State wildlife management agencies go by a wide variety of names, but searching for State Name + Fish and Game will usually bring up a link to the agency. Bear information can be challenging to find and is often not all in one location. Search for wildlife or living with wildlife on the home page or "living with bears" or "black bears." Go to the newsroom and see if you can sign up for alerts or newsletters. And email your agency and ask them to make living with wildlife information easier to find.

The following states offer in-depth information on living with bears.

Alaska Department of Fish and Game Division of Wildlife Conservation
www.wildlife.alaska.gov
Great info on all three species but it takes several clicks to find Living with Bears. Start with Wildlife then click on Living with Wildlife to start.

Colorado Parks and Wildlife
www.wildlife.state.co.us
In-depth resources plus a series of downloadable fact sheets cover some aspects of living and recreating in bear country not always addressed, including info for vacation homeowners, and a guide to electric fencing and unwelcome mats.

Florida Fish and Wildlife Conservation Commission
www.myfwc.com
Start with Wildlife Species on the Home Page, under Managed Species click on bears. Very comprehensive resources, including links to Florida's bear curriculum.

Kentucky Fish and Wildlife
www.fw.ky.gov
This information-packed website is worth the journey. Start with Wildlife on the home page, then choose Wildlife Home and then Bears. Comprehensive information and one of the most readable and down-to-earth question-and-answer sections.

Maine Dept. of Inland Fisheries and Wildlife
www.state.me.us/ifw
It takes a little digging, but you can find info on coexisting with bears.

Missouri Dept. of Conservation
www.conservation.state.mo.us
Black bears were nearly exterminated in Missouri, and are now making a comeback. Search Black Bears from the home page to find the black bear project and much more info.

Montana Fish Wildlife and Parks
www.fwp.mt.gov
Search for Bears and you'll find a trail cam gallery and lots of links to helpful information on both black and grizzly bears.

Nevada Dept. of Wildlife
www.ndow.org
Also provides links to sources for bear-resistant containers, county anti-feeding ordinances, electric fencing resources and Nevada's Karelian Bear Dog team.

Oregon Dept. of Fish & Wildlife
www.dfw.state.or.us
With a healthy bear population, Oregon offers lots of information and plenty of links, including some to other Sierra Nevada agencies.

Pennsylvania Game Commission State Wildlife Management Agency
www.dcnr.state.pa.us/
Good info if you search for bears.

Tennessee Wildlife Resources Agency
www.state.tn.us/twra
Well beyond the normal amount of information on black bears, plus extensive research data. The longest running study (39 years) of black bears was conducted in Great Smoky Mountains National Park.

Virginia Dept. of Fish and Game
www.dgif.virginia.gov
Comprehensive information including brochures, fact sheets, and videos on living with bears, making your own bear-resistant containers, how to use electric fencing to deter bears, plus info for beekeepers.

Washington Dept. of Fish and Wildlife
wdfw.wa.gov/living/bears.html
Lots of good information and an in-depth look at the agency's Karelian Bear Dog team at work (look under Enforcement or search for Karelian Bear Dogs).

Wyoming Game & Fish
www.gf.state.wy.us
Good grizzly bear info.

Canadian Agencies

Parks Canada
www.pc.gc.ca
You can find parks through this website, but info on living with bears is easier to find on the individual park websites.

Alberta Environment and Sustainable Resources Development
http://esrd.alberta.ca/recreation-public-use/alberta-bear-smart/
Lots of information, but hard to find. Search Alberta Bear Smart.

Manitoba
www.gov.mb.ca/conservation/wildlife
Good information, but hard to find. Look under Problem Wildlife or try searching "living with bears."

Ontario
www.mnr.gov.on.ca
A refreshingly user-friendly website with lots of good info. Search "living with bears" on the home page.

Yukon
www.environmentyukon.gov.yk.ca
Good info in English and French on black bears and safety in bear country. Start with wildlife species and follow the links. Click on Safety for lots of info.

Canadian Wildlife Federation
www.cwf-fcf.org
Polar bears, grizzly bears and black bears, but not as much information as you might expect.

GLOSSARY OF BEAR TERMS

anthropogenic food. Any source of calories that comes from humans or human activities, including but not limited to garbage, food, beverages, pet food, bees and honey, birdseed, grains, cultivated fruits, fish hatcheries, fish food, livestock and pets.

apiary. A place where bees and beehives are kept; generally a place where bees are raised for their honey.

attack. When a bear intentionally comes in contact with and injures a person.

attractant. Anything that draws a bear into an area, including natural foods (berries, nuts, ungulate carcasses), anthropogenic foods, or things that smell interesting but are not edible, such as motor oil, antifreeze, fertilizer and anything that gives off formic acid.

aversive conditioning. A structured program using noisemakers, trained dogs, projectiles, humans, or vehicles in response to a bear approaching or entering an area of human activity. Aversive conditioning stops when the bear returns to a natural area.

bearanoia. An irrational and unfounded fear that bears are out to get you. Perpetuated by folklore and the media.

bear jam. The traffic congestion that results when people stop along the road to watch or photograph bears. A common phenomena in areas where bears are protected and have become habituated to human activity.

bear manager. Often a bear biologist engaged in managing bear populations to ensure their long-term viability. Generally works for the state, federal or provincial government. Dealing with and preventing human-bear conflicts is usually part of the job.

bear management plan. A detailed long-term plan for setting objectives for bear populations and managing those populations to meet the objectives. Most states and provinces and some federal entities or interagency groups prepare management plans. Find plans on websites or by poking around on the Internet. They often contain detailed reviews of bear status, threats, opportunities, and actions needed.

bear researcher. A scientist studying various aspects of bear biology and/or behavior.

bear guy. The person expected to come and advise people on how to solve the problems they are having with bears. Bear guy is a unisex term. Lots of bear guys are women, sometimes referred to as bear ladies.

bear-resistant. Containers, devices or methods designed to keep bears out.

bear-resistant container (BRC). In the U.S., this refers to containers that have successfully passed the Interagency Grizzly Bear Committee's Bear Resistant Products Testing Protocol.

bear spray. Capsaicin spray specifically manufactured and EPA-approved for use on bears as a deterrent.

bluff charge. A bear charges a person or another bear, but does not make physical contact. Almost always defensive behavior meant to prevent a physical encounter.

boar. An adult male bear.

cub. Refers to a bear one year old or less. Black bears stay with their mothers until the spring following their birth, so they are about 12 to 18 months old when they go out on their own. Grizzly bears stay with their mothers much longer, until they are three or four years old (technically called subadults).

defensive behavior. The bear is responding to what it perceives as a threat to itself, a food source or cubs. Most bear attacks are defensive.

encounter. In bear terminology, it means the same as an interaction. Civilians tend to think that an interaction is a non-violent occasion involving bears and people, whereas an encounter is something unexpected or scary, but that's not what bear professionals mean when they describe human-bear activity.

euthanized. The polite way to describe killing a bear that's run out of chances, or poses a real or perceived threat to human safety. Civilians think of euthanasia as mercy killing done to put an animal out of its suffering. Most euthanized bears are perfectly healthy but are being killed to solve a problem that people created.

feeding bears. Refers to both intentionally and unintentionally providing any food source for bears.

food-conditioned bear. A bear that has learned that where there are people, there is food.

habituated bear. A bear that has learned to be "indifferent" to some sort of stimulus, whether it is the presence of people or flashing lights and noisemakers. Habituated bears are not necessarily food conditioned. Many bears in places with heavy human traffic, such as national parks, have become used to people in order to access natural food sources.

hibernation. A period of deep sleep/dormancy that can last anywhere from four to six months, depending on the bear's location and condition. Bears do not eat, urinate, or defecate during hibernation, but they do give birth to their cubs.

human-bear conflict. Includes interactions, encounters, and incidents in which there is a real or perceived threat to human life or property.

hyperphagia. A period during late summer and fall when bears go on an eating binge and consume up to 20,000 calories a day in order to gain enough weight before hibernation to survive the winter. Bears roam much farther than normal during hyperphagia, and feed up to 20 hours a day.

incident. An interaction between a bear and a person in which the bear acts aggressively. An incident can end peacefully or with an injury.

intentional feeding. Providing food for the express purpose of feeding or attracting wildlife, including bears. Illegal in many communities, states and provinces.

IBA, International Association for Bear Research and Management. Formerly the International Bear Association, it is the leading professional organization for bear managers and researchers.

Karelian Bear Dog (KBD). Trained KBDs are used in aversive conditioning, as well as research, searching, locating and law enforcement.

lethal control. Killing a bear that poses a real or perceived threat to human safety or property.

management bear. Typically refers to an individual bear that is being monitored. It could be the recipient of many types of management, from simple observation to attempts to deter the bear from human areas to interventions, like aversive conditioning or relocation.

non-lethal management. Employs various tools such as aversive conditioning, translocation and relocation in order to deter bears from human areas or stop potentially harmful behavior without having to kill the bear.

nuisance bear. Another term similar to 'problem bear' that needs to be eradicated from our vocabulary. Often used to describe a bear that is involved in human-bear interactions that are annoying, but don't pose a real threat to human safety. Blames the bear instead of holding people accountable for causing the problem.

nuisance human. Person who intentionally engages in behavior that attracts bears to home, property, camp, or elsewhere bears should not be.

NGO. Non-government organizations often partner with government agencies in efforts to improve human-bear relations.

offensive behavior. The bear's behavior is not in response to a real or perceived threat. True offensive behavior is rare.

on-site or hard release. Capturing a bear (usually one involved in human-bear conflicts) and releasing it at the site of the capture accompanied by yelling, chasing with dogs, noisemakers, and other methods meant to teach the bear to avoid the site in the future.

overt reaction distance. A fancy scientific term for invading a bear's personal comfort zone. It's the distance at which a bear's behavior changes in response to another bear, a disturbance of some type, or a person.

predatory bear. The very rare bear that has or has attempted to prey on people.

problem bear. A term that professionals use to describe a bear that requires some sort of management action, ranging from simple monitoring to lethal removal. Civilians think this means that the bear is causing the problem, while generally the opposite is true.

relocation. Capturing a bear in one area and moving it somewhere else within its home range. Often done in a conflict situation to buy time so that attractants can be removed and bear-proofing can be instituted.

sighting. You see a bear, but the bear doesn't appear to see you.

sow. An adult female bear.

stakeholder. Any group, person, organization or entity that has a stake in the outcome of an issue. Government speak for all the various factions that must be considered every time they do something.

subadult. A young bear of either sex that is not sexually mature. Usually between one and three years old.

translocation. Capturing a bear in one area and moving it outside of its home range in hopes it will settle down in a new area.

ungulate. Technically all manner of hooved mammals, including horses, mules and zebras. Wild ungulates include deer, elk and moose.

unintentional feeding. You didn't mean to feed the bears, but you did anyway, by providing accessible garbage, food, birdseed, pet food, fruits, nuts, berries or anything else that attracts bears. Illegal in many states and provinces.

Ursus americanus. The North American black bear.

Ursus arctos. The brown bear, found in Europe, Asia and Russia as well as in coastal Canada and Alaska.

Ursus arctos horribilis. The grizzly bear; found in a few western states, Canada and interior Alaska.

Ursus arctos middendorffi. A subspecies of brown bear found only in the Kodiak archipelago, commonly known as the Kodiak bear, and one of the largest bears in the world.

Ursus urbanus: A term coined by author Linda Masterson to describe bears in urban areas that have become almost totally dependent on human-provided food sources like garbage. They grow bigger, have more cubs, and lead much shorter lives than wild bears.

National Park Service, Yosemite National Park

ACKNOWLEDGMENTS

I wish I could personally thank everyone who helped bring this second edition of *Living With Bears* to life. I started working on it in 2010; in 2011 a wildfire destroyed my Colorado home and everything I owned, including my research library. I lost all my paper references along with stacks of business cards, so if you helped me out and I failed to say thanks, at least you know why.

My incredibly talented, insightful and doggedly persistent publisher LaVonne Ewing and my scientific and real-world bear barometer Rich Beausoleil stuck with me through it all. I often wonder if Rich had any clue what he was getting himself into when he agreed to help me make sure the information in this book was biologically impeccable and real-world practical. If he had called up my original bear barometer Tom Beck, he might have tossed in the towel. But he persisted, and was somehow never too busy to help (Rich once sent me comments from a snowmobile trip to check den sites). He read and commented on every word and every revision, and his experience, knowledge and attention to both detail and the big picture helped make this a much better and more useful book.

And many thanks to the bear biologists and researchers who also reviewed and commented on the manuscript, including Steve Herrero, Hank Hristienko, Rachel Mazur, Colleen Olfenbuttel, Jaime Sajecki, Carl Lackey, Dave Telesco, John Hechtel and Larry Van Daele.

Bear researchers, biologists and managers are, by and large (often with good reason), cautious about working with anyone lacking an alphabet soup of scientific credentials. Many have been misquoted often enough to develop a natural wariness of the media. But at the same time they all know that nurturing good relations with good people is the best way to spread the good word. So I'm proud of the long list of bear folks who trusted me enough to share their wealth of knowledge and experiences. Their voices help these pages ring true.

Regarded as the world's leading authority on bear encounters and attacks, University of Calgary professor and bear researcher Steve Herrero reviewed and helped me fine-tune the information on bear behavior, encounters and attacks. Thankfully Great Smoky Mountains National Park's Supervisory Wildlife Biologist Bill Stiver has not adopted government-speak as his primary language, and was as much help on this edition as on the first one when he was the park's "bear guy." Virginia's Black Bear Project Leader Jaime Sajecki is an inspiring example of a new breed of bear managers focused on both parts of the human-bear equation. When I met Rachel Mazur she was the bear biologist at Kings Canyon National Park; today she's a published author and wildlife conflicts expert with Yosemite National Park. Florida's Dave Telesco helped me unravel the long and complicated journey back from the brink for Florida's black bears.

The Kodiak Archipelago's Larry Van Daele helped me better understand these giants of the bear world. Manitoba's Hank Hristienko patiently worked me through the intricacies of bear nutritional requirements. Minnesota's Karen Noyce helped me tell the story of the oldest known black bear. Yellowstone's Kerry Gunther provided much thoughtful research and advice, and changed the way I thought about bear jams. North Carolina's bear biologist Colleen Olfenbuttel lent a unique perspective that helped me fine-tune.

The Get Bear Smart Society's knowledgeable, committed and tireless director Sylvia Dolson was always ready to help. Chuck Bartlebaugh, who now runs the Be Bear Aware Classroom on Wheels, gave me the world's most painstakingly thorough lesson on the finer points of bear spray. North Carolina State University's Professor of Entomology David Tarpy solved the mystery of how many calories there are in a hive full of bee brood and beekeeper Jay Bradshaw documented his journey to bear-proof beekeeping. Kootenay Tribal biologist George Barce shared how he managed to do something many bear guys only dream about—get hundreds of garbage containers painlessly switched over to bear-resistant ones.

I owe thanks to more people than I can mention in my former home state of Colorado, including Parks and Wildlife district wildlife managers Kevin Wright and Jim Jackson, education coordinator Mary McCormac, and my fellow Bear Aware volunteers, especially Jim and Jane Tiffin who led the charge at Crystal Lakes and the indefatigable Donna Forrest, along with Snowmass officers Laurie Smith and Tina White and large carnivore biologist Jerry Apker.

I have a writer's admiration for NPS Interpreter Malinee Crapsey, Northern Cascades bear biologist Anne Braaten, and Colorado District Wildlife Manager Chris Parmeter, whose own words make their points even more convincingly than I could.

The book has greatly benefited from the many bear experts whose work presented at conferences and in scientific journals provided invaluable information and whose stories shared added great insights, including Carl Lackey, Chris Servheen, Dave Garshelis, Marty Obbard, Jamie Jonkel, Chuck Jonkel, Carrie Hunt, John Beecham, John Hechtel, Jon Beckmann, Sean Mathews, Michael Pelton and conflict prevention specialists Kim Tichener and Patti Sowka.

Many professional photographers lent us their photos because they believed in the cause, as did countless bear enthusiasts. Others repeatedly dug through their files or helped us unearth images, including Rich Beausoleil, Carl Lackey, Larry Van Daele, Bill Stiver, Gary Alt, Caitlin Lee-Roney, Kerry Gunther, Malinee Crapsee, Anne Braaten, Jaime Sajecki, Sylvia Dolson and Jeffrey Trust.

Special thanks go out to Smoky Mountains' extraordinary volunteer Warren Bielenberg, who made several 90-mile round trips to capture their bear programs in action. And big bear hugs are in order for illustrator Sara Tuttle; don't miss the drolly accurate new Anthropogenic Food beartoon she created just for this edition.

I wish I could thank every one of the people who helped with the first edition all over again. Especially now-retired bear biologist Tom Beck, who spent a billion hours helping me and persuaded many of his harried colleagues to do likewise, and insightful, helpful and well-connected wildlife conflict prevention specialist Patti Sowka.

I could never have written this book without the unflagging support of my husband Cory, who did more than his share of just about everything while I was up to my ears in bears, and the occasional pile of bear scat.

Finally, my deepest thanks to everyone who bought and read and re-read and post-it noted, passed around, recommended and really used the first edition. You can now safely retire it, because this one is even better.

BIBLIOGRAPHY

My background as a writer and researcher and Rich Beausoleil's science- and fact-driven approach to bear management made us eager to include the extensive bibliography for this edition in the book. But in the end we decided the many pages required would be better used imparting more practical information on living with bears and reducing human-bear conflicts. So you'll find the complete bibliography on my website, *www.LivingWithBears.com.*

The nature of this book involved the review of hundreds of scientific papers and many books along with hundreds of websites, bear informational brochures, and newspaper and magazine articles far too numerous to list. I reviewed all state agency and provincial websites and many state bear management plans. I interviewed and/or corresponded with hundreds of people involved in bear management, education and conservation throughout North America.

Sources with numerous citations include:

Ursus, the official publication of the International Association for Bear Research and Management (IBA)

International Bear News, IBA's quarterly newsletter

Proceedings of numerous IBA conferences

Proceedings of Eastern and Western Black Bear workshops

The Journal of Wildlife Management

Wildlife Conservation Society

U.S. Fish and Wildlife Service

U.S. Forest Service

U.S. National Park Service

Canadian Bear Smart Community protocols

INDEX

TECHNICAL ADVISOR

RICH BEAUSOLEIL

Rich Beausoleil has been conducting bear research since 1997 in Louisiana, Tennessee, New Mexico and Washington, where he's been the statewide bear and cougar specialist for the Washington Department of Fish and Wildlife since 2002. He's the Chair of the Management Committee for the International Association for Bear Research and Management (IBA) and a frequent contributor to professional publications and journals. He's also authored several agency manuals on responding to human-carnivore conflicts, and his efforts contributed to the state of Washington passing an anti-feeding regulation.

Rich cofounded the Karelian Bear Dog (KBD) Program in Washington in 2003, and has more than a decade of experience as a handler, using KBD's to help resolve conflict between bears and people non-lethally. He's a frequent speaker at both professional conferences and community events, although he freely admits that understanding bears is often much easier than unraveling the mysteries of human behavior. He holds double degrees in wildlife biology, a BS from the University of Massachusetts at Amherst and a Master's Degree from the University of Tennessee at Knoxville.

AUTHOR

LINDA MASTERSON

photo by Desariah Santillanez

Author and researcher Linda Masterson has always believed that you catch more bears—and readers—with honey than you do with vinegar. Her award-winning work has appeared in the *New York Times* Sunday magazine, *Animal Kingdom, Ranger Rick, New Pioneer, Log Home Living* and many others. She is a frequent and popular speaker, and has been a featured presenter at various International Bear Management Association conferences and workshops.

She was a member of Colorado Parks and Wildlife's Bear Aware team for more than a decade. Linda and husband Cory Phillips spend as much time outdoors as possible, and have explored more than a hundred parks and forests in the U.S. and Canada. She's a partner in marketing and communications firm Masterson & Phillips and lives on Florida's southern Gulf Coast.

www.LivingWithBears.com

ALSO BY LINDA:

Surviving Wildfire:
Get Prepared, Stay Alive, Rebuild Your Life
(A Handbook for Homeowners)

LivingWithBears.com

Please visit our website for a wealth of information:

- ❖ Beary-Smart Solutions for homeowners, HOAs and resort communities, municipalities, and organizations.
- ❖ Tested outreach ideas for bear managers, wildlife agencies, parks and forests, campgrounds, educators, volunteers and interpreters.
- ❖ Guidelines for electric fencing, and electric and conventional unwelcome mats.
- ❖ Sample no-feeding and conflict-prevention ordinances.
- ❖ Links to photographers' websites.
- ❖ Book reviews, testimonials, full bibliography, and media materials.
- ❖ Wholesale ordering information for groups, organizations or anyone who needs an educational / outreach tool, a fundraising item, or welcome / thank you gifts.

© Sara Tuttle

Visit **PixyJackPress.com** to view all of our wildlife and nature titles.

Made in the USA
Columbia, SC
11 September 2020